Spiritual Gifts: Discovering and Using them

Chris A. Legebow

Living Word

ISBN: 978-0-9952715-0-0
CANADA

DEDICATION

I dedicate this book to the Body of Christ. May you as a Christian know your purpose and your gifts and talents and use them for God's glory. Live your life doing all that you do to glorify Christ.   I thank God for the local churches I have been a part of. Thank you to the numerous ministries that teach and preach and broadcast Christ through all forms of Media.

May the Apostles , Prophets, Evangelists, Teachers, and Pastors as well as the servants , givers, exhorters, leaders, and mercies be used to build up the Body of Christ.

Forward

It is my hope and my prayer that God will encourage you with this book help you to discover and use your motivational spiritual gifts. Please know there is so much more about spiritual gifts that could be written because we are constantly discovering fresh ways God is using people.

May God also help you to learn about other people's spiritual gifts so you can understand those with different giftings than yourself. May you always realize that God gets the glory; He placed those gifts and talents in you; He uses you by prompting you in your spirit and He manifest the results of the gifts. He gets all the glory. God is the author and finisher of your faith.

This book was written to share with you ways that God can and does use His people.

With Christian love and prayer

Chris Legebow

Chris A. Legebow

CONTENTS

ACKNOWLEDGMENTS

All Scripture taken from Biblegateway,com
King James Version (KJV)
Modern English Version (MEV)
New International Version (NIV)
.

CHAPTER 1
INTRODUCTION TO MOTIVATIONAL GIFTS

Most young people have enthusiasm, energy and passion. Sometimes they know their direction and often they do not. One reason I would write this book is to help people of all ages discover their spiritual gifts and encourage them to use them. The gifts are usually discussed by these three categories: Motivational. Manifestational and Ministry. (Bill Gauthier)

The purpose of this book is to help you recognize your motivational gifts, to know more about them and to be encouraged to use them. I recommend that people should be taught about spiritual gifts as soon as they have come to Christ as part of a teaching on the foundations. Personally, I would emphasize these gifts after water baptism or a serious commitment to Christ. Truly there is no age group these truths do not apply to. The believers should be taught that they have gifts and talents and that God has a purpose for their lives which would include using the gifts and talents for His glory.

Spiritual gifts are used by the Body of Christ within the Church. They are used to build up, strengthen and encourage the members of the Body of Christ. They are also used outside of the physical church building to encourage Christians and to glorify God, often in Evangelism. Literally, we Christians believe we are the hands and feet of Jesus on the earth: that is He lives in us and the Holy Spirit, who dwells in us, will use us through the giftings He gives us. As unique as a person's DNA, so unique is the combination of spiritual giftings. It is important to know the giftings and to be instructed in the operation of the giftings.

Gifts for a purpose

Spiritual gifts are important for you in the Body of Christ and also for you as a minister of reconciliation as you witness about Christ and lead others to come to know Him. Every Christian is called to be a minister of reconciliation. Jesus commanded us to go and make disciples. That means we should be sharing Christ with others; the gifts often are used to help us in both witnessing and demonstrating the glory of God; this includes our home, our spheres of influence and in direct ministry opportunities.

1 Corinthians 12: 4-11 (MEV Bible Gateway)

4 There are various gifts, but the same Spirit. 5 There are differences of administrations, but the same Lord. 6 There are various operations, but it is the same God who operates all of them in all people. 7 But the manifestation of the Spirit is given to everyone for the common good. 8 To one is given by the Spirit the word of wisdom, to another the word of knowledge by the same Spirit, 9 to another faith by the same Spirit, to another gifts of healings by the same Spirit, 10 to another the working of miracles, to another prophecy, to another discerning of spirits, to another various kinds of tongues, and to another the interpretation of tongues. 11 But that one and very same Spirit works all these, dividing to each one individually as He will.

To examine this passage more closely, the Bible says there are many types of gifts but they are all from the same Holy Spirit. The Holy Spirit living in you expresses Himself through you, through gifts, through fruit, through character. Not all spiritual gifts flow exactly the same way, the same level or the same measure.

Motivational Gifts

I would compare the depths of the essence of Spiritual gifts to literal space without limit so that in such a way, in can not be measured. The magnitude of our own universe is hard to comprehend but the truth of other universes truly makes us seem small in comparison. I would ask you to imagine that space so tremendous and the love of God filling that space, saturating that space with His presence; He wants to reach people. What He does is He gives us Spiritual gifts into our very essence, our being as we are first conceived in our mother's womb.

The person is designed to use those gifts and talents and abilities. After a person is born again, filled with the Holy Spirit, those gifts become unlocked. God is able to speak to us directly and literally flow through us – to touch others. Before we become born again Christians, we had a spirit but it was all shrivelled up like a wrinkled dry balloon. This is a direct result of the sin of Adam. (see note: Adam and Eve knew direct communion with God until they sinned. Once they sinned, their spirits which once knew God's direct presence became dry and shrivelled. Original sin entered the world and the spirit is never fully used until a person is born again. Once we are born again, the Spirit of God fills our spirit and it becomes like a balloon filled with air – only it is our spirit which can now function by giving and receiving from the spirit realm – God's presence fills us)

Living in the Spirit

We should be living in the Spirit no matter what the position in life: a student, a farmer, a teacher, a doctor, a truck driver etc. There were early Americans who believed this and actually came to the North America to live Holy lives. They came wanting to find spiritual freedom. These Shakers and Quakers and Amish people lived a simple life but believed they could commune with God in the everyday activities, throughout the day as well as in services on Sunday. They lived prayerfully even though they were doing ordinary tasks. They knew the presence of God in their lives. They used their gifts and talents in the ordinary as well as in the church buildings.

What I am saying is that we can live in the spirit and operate in the spirit even though we have a secular job. We should use the education and training we have received but always be communing with God to ask for help and guidance throughout our day. God wants to be a partner with us in our lives, in everything we do: work, school, home, society etc. People say God has a plan for your life, but they never continue with it. Part of that plan is to reveal Himself to you uniquely as His creation, including all spiritual gifts and talents. It is true, God does have a plan, but you must cooperate with the plan.

How God Uses Us

If we do not cooperate with the Holy Spirit, He will not force us. His plan will not be accomplished unless we not only yield but desire to be filled with God's presence and used by God to minister to others. God speaks to us, spirit to spirit. Our born again spirit filled spirit is the dwelling place for the Holy Spirit within us. As we meditate on the things of God, as we worship God, as we praise God, God fills our being. With this indwelling, comes a release of the giftings of the LORD and revelation and wisdom on how to use the gifts.

Upon the Baptism of the Holy Spirit, there is a whole new realm of operation. A new level of existence is available to us. I would compare it to an overflow. The container not only filled to the brim but overflowing with no end in sight. The Holy Spirit empowers us for a purpose: it is to accomplish the will of God in the earth.

Connection with the Holy Spirit is important to be used by God but if you do not know the gifts that you have, you won't even think of using them. You will not be living to your full potential because you do not even know what you have. This is the main reason I want to speak about spiritual gifts, so people may press in to know Jesus more, so that people will know their giftings, so that people will use their giftings to glorify God.

Psalm 139 (MEV Bible Gateway)

13 You brought my inner parts into being;
You wove me in my mother's womb.
14 I will praise you, for You made me with fear and wonder;
marvelous are Your works, and You know me completely.

God literally created you. You were in the mind of God before you were placed in your mother's womb. God chose your family. God chose your generation. God chose to bring you to your parents. If you have never read any of Bill Gauthaurd 's Basic Institute for Life or been to any of his seminars, get some information on his teachings concerning how God created you as you are: with your spiritual DNA, hair colour size etc. It is especially excellent concerning accepting yourself and your purpose as a gift from God. It is an excellent teaching and there are excellent textbooks that go along with it.

The same God who created all of the universe and created all things that exist – created you with such intricate, careful design that He wanted to put His signature on you saying that you were made in His image and likeness. God literally designed you the way you are so He could reveal His glory through you. God knew what our gifts and talents would be like, our gifts, our talents, our choices, our vocation.

Psalm 139: 15 My frame was not hidden from You
when I was made in secret,
and intricately put together in the lowest parts of the earth.
16 Your eyes saw me unformed,
yet in Your book
all my days were written,
before any of them came into being.

Just as there are millions of cells in the human body, God knew every one of them. God knows every possible aspect of our lives: past, present and future. I am in awe of the God of creation who created all things but cared so much that He made me on purpose, who loved me before I ever knew Him, who died for me over 2, 000 years ago so that I could be saved. He cared for me, wooed me to Himself, caused me to come to know Him. He forgave me, filled me, Baptized me with the Holy Spirit. He directs my steps and teaches me, lovingly guiding me. He gave me gifts and talents that I might be a co-labourer together with Him that I might accomplish His will on the earth. Please – this truth is no for me only – it is for you; it is for you; it is for you.

1 Corinthinas 12: 7 But the manifestation of the Spirit is given to everyone for the common good. 8 To one is given by the Spirit the word of wisdom, to another the word of knowledge by the same Spirit, 9 to another faith by the same Spirit, to another gifts of healings by the same Spirit, 10 to another the working of miracles, to another prophecy, to another discerning of spirits, to another various kinds of tongues, and to another the interpretation of tongues. 11 But that one and very same Spirit works all these, dividing to each one individually as He will.

The Holy Spirit gives to every person a measure of the gifts: to profit the person to profit the body of Christ and to accomplish the will of God on the earth. These are the manifestation; gifts. They are the topic of a different study but for our purposes they will be mentioned as they are used and are evident as we use our Motivational gifts.

Words of wisdom
Words of knowledge
Discerning of spirits
Faith
Healing gifts
Working of miracles
Prophecy
Tongues
Interpretation of tongues

You are Unique

Although there are all these different giftings, there is one Spirit – and all the gifts are from Him. How God manifests Himself in you and through you is as unique as your finger prints – no two people are identical. To every person is given to them, gifts – unique to shine through him or her as a gem shines the light in manifold ways; the Holy Spirit shines through us – as we use our gifts and talents in manifold ways.

The Body of Christ

Later in the Scripture the Apostle Paul gives the analogy specific as the Body of Christ as a human body – arms, legs, torso etc. He explains the function of hand is completely different than the function of the feet or the ears or the eyes but all parts are necessary for the person to be whole. There are no extra parts in a human body. Every part has a different but precise function.

The systems of the body are fascinating; our circulatory system is totally different than our respiratory system. All of the systems of the body work together to help us run, and jump, dance, and do normal and spectacular things.

You have a specific place and function in The Body of Christ: each part of the body contributes something to the body. Parts help each other and work together. As a human body grows and develops from infancy to adulthood, so too does the local Body of Christ grow as parts of the body help and work together with other parts of the body. Example, a baby does not have motor control over his or her hands and legs. As the child grows, mastery of using the parts of the body is accomplished. The child can grasp, crawl, walk etc. A baby may grasp your finger trying to communicate and comprehend you. Later, he or she can manipulate objects. As the child grows, gross motor and fine motor skills are developed.

Spiritual Gifts develop as you Exercise them

Spiritual gifts grow by exercising them. Please listen to what I said. You must exercise them. You must use the gifts in order for them to grow. A person who is a surgeon or dentist or craftsman or jeweler can use his or her hands in a precise way with accuracy and skill. I am saying God wants us to develop our gifts with skill, precision and accuracy so they can precisely be applied to people's lives, to build up or strengthen the body of Christ or to lead others to the saving knowledge of Christ.

Christ lives in You

Of course you have the seed of all the gifts of the Spirit within in because Christ lives in you; Christ is not divided. But each person has a different measure – some stronger in some areas than others, usually 2 or 3 or 4 predominate ones. If Christ lives in you, all the gifts are there. We usually operate with certain giftings in certain spheres of influence in our lives but if you were to be the only Christian in a situation where a particular gift was needed, and it wasn't one of your main giftings, God could and would use you in that situation. God gives gifts to different people for different reasons. God doesn't give you gifts so you could showcase your gifts and say these are my gifts – and they sit there on the shelf. He doesn't give us gifts so we can hide them either. Placing them in a storage area to dust off and use occasionally is not what He wills for us either. He doesn't give us gifts so we can keep them to ourselves either.

These are the ministry gifts, the fivefold ministry of the body of Christ.

Ephesians 4: 11 He gave some to be apostles, prophets, evangelists, pastors, and teachers, 12 for the equipping of the saints, for the work of service, and for the building up of the body of Christ,12 for the equipping of the saints, for the work of service, and for the building up of the body of Christ, 13 until we all come into the unity of the faith and of the knowledge of the Son of God, into a complete man, to the measure of the stature of the fullness of Christ, 14 so we may no longer be children, tossed here and there by waves and carried about with every wind of doctrine by the trickery of men, by craftiness with deceitful scheming. 15 But, speaking the truth in love, we may grow up in all things into Him, who is the head, Christ Himself, 16 from whom the whole body is joined together and connected by every joint and ligament, as every part effectively does its work and grows, building itself up in love.

Certainly the fivefold ministry is essential to the building up, equipping and training fo the saints. They will be mentioned in relationship to motivational gifts in this study.

The ministry gifts are given to us so they can sharpen all the other giftings in the church, The Apostles, Prophets, Pastors, Teachers, Evangelists are to help perfect us and mature us for the work of the ministry. We are the doers of the ministry. The ministry gifts teach us, equip us and assist us in using our gifts. I can reach people in spheres of influence that others cannot. You can reach others in spheres of your influence that others cannot. Together, we are the Body of Christ global and local. We are to live our lives so that we can affect people in all spheres of our lives.

If there are no spiritual gifts in the church in manifestation, that is a sign that the church is not doing well. If there is life in the church, spiritual gifts are evident in the church.

The 7 Mountains

The evidence of life in the spirit is the manifestation of the gifts of the spirit in the Church. Youth with a Mission Loren Cunningham defined 7 spheres of influence in society for us. I got the teaching from Lance Wallnau. If you have not heard of his teachings on this topic, I highly recommend you watch or listen as it is excellent for Market place ministry or ministry outside the literal church building

.

The 7 spheres include the following:

Arts (music, dance, graphic arts, painting, plays, movies, books, poetry etc.) and Entertainment

Media (newspapers, satellite, tv, world news communication systems of all kinds)

Church and religion

Politics

Education

Business

Family

I would add to this list:

Science and Technology , health care

Ministering in the Marketplace

These spheres of influence are natural but we need not be natural in them. For instance, if you are a business person, you carry Christ with you into your place of Business. We should be doing our best as unto Christ in everything we do; our words, our service, our sincere care for the people we are with should be evident. Be should be asking God for wisdom to do our natural jobs, drawing from His Holy Spirit.

Oh. how dare we think that we don't need God in our jobs. God cares about you mowing the lawn. Listening to God could make the difference between you being safe or chopping off your finger. We should remain spiritually in communion with God throughout our day no matter what we are doing. Talking to God, given to prayer and relying on The Holy Spirit to teach us and help us are important not only for our own welfare but so that we can minister to the people around us. We are meant to live in the spirit realm; that means God may give you a word of wisdom while you are doing an ordinary task. God could place someone on your heart to pray for at any point in your day – or even in your dreams.

Spiritual Living

We should be spiritually ready to hear from God with an attitude of prayer, praise, thanksgiving always – without ceasing; yes, I know it isn't always humanly true – but that is my aim. The Apostle Paul encouraged us to pray without ceasing. I literally believe he lived his life that way. I aim to live my life with that goal in sight – living for God with all my being. God can give us inside information, wisdom to solve problems, wisdom to apply knowledge or technique. God living in us calls us co-labourers together with Him. God with us in life – not only the gifts and talents He has given us.

Get Education and Training

In those spheres of influence God will use our education and training and gifts and talents. Please listen, God wants to use you and can use you in your sphere of influence but the more we do in terms of degrees and diplomas and certifications. The more opportunities become possible for us. Those are doors to a possible career and spheres of influence you could have on earth. We should aim to get as much education and training in areas of interest to us, as much as possible. Behind each one of the possible opportunities there are people and destiny decisions there. There are hundreds of people there, maybe thousands depending on your spheres of influence and your career etc. You could be influencing those people for Christ.

Spheres of Influence

For instance, a factory worker has an influence of maybe 200 people or more. These would be people in your work place and in the spheres of your work place. A teacher may have influence over thousands, depending on his or her teaching career and level of teaching and how many people they teach. So… it differs from person to person; it is unique. Your life is unique; it is important. You have a chance to use your life to be an expression of His glory and to honour Him with your life. We are ambassadors of God. We carry Him with us. Our motivational gifts lead us to doors of decision and influence.

It doesn't mean we have to be weird. We don't have to set up a shrine on our desk with tracts and get to know Jesus cards (in a secular job, it is not appropriate in current North American society).

I am not saying we shouldn't try to be witnesses, but we must use wisdom and rely on the Holy Spirit. It's our reliance on the Holy Spirit that makes us supernatural. It is the Jesus factor.

There is natural talent, education, training, certificates, spheres of influence, family background, etc. Ohhh… but then there is Jesus. The supernatural aspect of our lives – God Himself who wants to use us and will us in ways we would not know without His leading and prompting.

What I am saying is the Jesus factor – lifts us up to a higher level. We are not confined by our education or training or lack of it. God can use you in many types of situations. We are never confined by the things of earth. There are constraints on the earth – yes – but we have supernatural insight, given to us by God; we need to tap into getting it. We must position ourselves in a posture of communion with God. We should use our spiritual gifts in the areas He has given to us.

I have had opportunity to learn about my spiritual gifts early in my Christian life. Thank God, shortly after I became a Christian, I got some excellent teaching. It became a strong area of interest to me because I knew how important it was to my own life. I have read book after book on it so that I might be able to share with others that they too might know their giftings and use them. It is completely fascinating to me – the uniqueness of each person, how God created us differently, alike in some ways, different in so many ways. It is unique how expresses Himself as love to each person and through each person. Listening to someone's testimony shows how God uniquely brought that person into the light. You know your own self that God made the situation exactly right for you to accept Him as Saviour.

If you are a born-again spirit filled Christian you should be living in the realm above human capacity. You were raised on earth as a human but the new birth gives us a capacity for the supernatural. We have access to the resources of Heaven, the exclusive resources of Jesus Christ.

Spheres of Influence

Mostly you are called to one or two of those spheres of influence. Example, I have known pastors who are secular teachers by day, and pastors of churches. There are people who are in secular business, excellent in publishing and business and all matters of finance, but also are pastors. What I am saying is God can use you in ministry as well as in the secular realm. Don't believe the lie that you must choose between the two. We are all called to ministry – but not all of us are called to the five-fold ministry. Pray over the spheres of influence you are in. Pray for blessing on those people you interact with and also those in governmental positions and in authority. Pray that God would use you to light the way in your spheres of influence.

If you are a young person and don't have a job yet, it is so important that you get teaching about your spiritual gifts so that you know God cares about your life. God cares about your future. God wants you to have the best. If you have been baptized with the Holy Spirit, you must embrace the truth that God who filled you with His Spirit wants to give you the best in every area of your life.

Fear of God's Callings

I've spoken to some people who believe the lie that God wants something for you that you yourself hate or find repulsive. Example, I've spoken with some who say something like God will probably put me in some remote village in a mud hut in Africa where I don't want to go. These people are really doubting that God's love for them is perfect. You need to repent for not knowing God. The God that would ask you to go would give you the want to go also.

If you even doubt that God would want to give you the best possible, you must have your mind renewed. Romans 12: 1-2 (MEV Bible Gateway)

12 I urge you therefore, brothers, by the mercies of God, that you present your bodies as a living sacrifice, holy, and acceptable to God, which is your reasonable service of worship. 2 Do not be conformed to this world, but be transformed by the renewing of your mind, that you may prove what is the good and acceptable and perfect will of God.

Transformation of your View about God

Even though our spirit is immediately reborn, our mind must be transformed by God's Word and God's spirit. Only the combination of Word and Spirit can transform a soul (mind, will and emotions). The more we are in His presence, praying, praising, worshipping, reading the Word of God, gathered with saints in Word services etc. and the more we set ourselves towards God, the more He will transform us – from glory to glory.

A person who has been transformed by God knows that God only wants the best for us. He gave us the desires we have and it is His pleasure to give us the desires of our hearts. Those things that give us joy, like using our gifts and talents – He placed them into our being – He created us with those desires: to teach, to dance, to sing etc. It has been built in us to love to do these things. That is the God I serve – He knit into our very being the things that we would love and He delights to give us those opportunities to express His glory by being excellent at them.

Free Will

Jehovah will never go against your human will. That's why you had to receive Him as Saviour and LORD. He would never force you to accept Him and He will never force you to be baptized or Baptized with the Holy Spirit. He is a God who cares that your decision for Him be self-determined. Literally, you must ask Him to teach you and present yourself teachable so that you can learn about spiritual gifts, or anything else. Begin to pray, God grow me; I want to serve You; use me. We ought to say LORD, here I am; I present myself to You a living sacrifice; teach me: fill me; use me. Stay in a humble attitude of prayer.

The frequency of Hearing from God

If we do not actively pursue God with our being, God may whisper to us to speak to someone or pray for someone, but if we are dull spiritually, not active for God, we may not understand its importance and lives may depend on it. With the spheres of influence, comes spheres of authority and responsibility. God will speak to you spirit to spirit: His Spirit speaking with your spirit. If you are not living in your spirit, you will not be on the same frequency as God. God doesn't speak to your mind, will or emotions – He speaks Spirit to spirit.

He will impress on your spirit to use your gifts and talents. He wants to use us while we are on the earth. God mostly uses people. We pray, "Your kingdom come, Your will be done on earth as it is in heaven …" God mostly uses people to bring it to pass. He could use angels and He has. He could appear in person face to face, and He sometime does; mostly God uses the Body of Christ. He uses us on the earth to be agents of righteousness. Please know that if we neglect our spiritual lives and are hardened to Him, God will use someone else. He could and has used animals if necessary.

The High Call of God

We are to do the will of God and to bring the kingdom of God every place we go in all spheres of society. He wants us to do excellently, exceeding expectations, Oh yes, living for the high calling of God for our lives. The high calling is living for the purpose for which you were created – using all the gifts and talents and education and training – to shine the light of Christ into the spheres of society you connect and to develop those gifts and talents to the fullest potential possible.

The Apostle Paul

The story of the Apostle Paul getting saved is a supernatural story. It is the realm we are to live in. Please realize the Apostle Paul was fervent; he was diligent; he was educated he was zealous; he was passionate – but he was not serving God. In fact, he set himself to assist in the rounding up and killing of Christians because he did not believe they served God. He was 100% zealous Pharisee – going the wrong way. He used all within his sphere of influence but to literally oppose God – and he didn't know it.

God literally apprehended Saul; he never knew Jesus during Jesus life on the earth, but he met Jesus afterwards. He was literally going on a road with signed orders to kill Christians when he was apprehended by Jesus Himself. In the middle of his journey, he saw a bright light – so bright and so overwhelming that it knocked him to the ground and he was blinded by it. He heard the voice of the LORD saying Paul why do you persecute me? And Paul answered who are you LORD? And Jesus answered and said "I am Jesus whom you persecute."

Acts 9: 5 He said, "Who are You, Lord? "The Lord said, "I am Jesus, whom you are persecuting. It is hard for you to kick against the goads." 6 Trembling and astonished, he said, "Lord, what will You have me do?" The Lord said to him, "Rise up and go into the city, and you will be told what you must do."

God's Assignment for the Apostle Paul

It is so possible to be religious and not know God. Jesus appeared to Saul in person. God appears to him and tells him he will be a living witness for God – before he even was saved. Saul accepts it and knows it is God. It is a radical shift in his life – totally radical. He was transformed from one way of believing to a totally different belief by the revelation of the person of Jesus Christ.

He had been teaching only the Jewish laws and beliefs to Jews only but suddenly he finds out he was fighting against the Messiah Jesus. In Fact, Jesus told him he would bring the gospel of salvation to the Gentiles. Most of the Gentiles were completely lost, serving pagan gods – not serving the God of Israel. God explains His purposes for Saul's life and Saul's response is what would you have me to do LORD? He is willing and obedient.

God literally gives him directions that involve his obedience and the obedience of others. He was told the street to go to. He was told Ananias would come and lay hands on him and pray for him and he would be healed. He obeyed and fasted and prayed until Ananias came. The experience in the supernatural was so strong it not only healed him but made him a passionate preacher of Jesus Christ the Messiah in the very synagogues he would have gone to - to persecute Christians.

God sent Ananias to speech to Saul and pray for him. It is not something Ananias wanted to do because he knew Saul was a killer of Christians. He had supernatural insight from God. He greets Saul "Brother, Saul". Ananias believed God and acted in faith praying for Paul. These spiritual gifts can help us to help others in a similar way. God can instruct us as much as we are willing to give ourselves.

What is your response to God's Callings?

His response is like the response of the Virgin Mary. When angels appeared to the Virgin Mary announcing that she will become the mother of the Messiah – she says " Be it unto me according to your will." She comes into agreement.

They both immediately got their lives in line with the will of God realizing there is a higher purpose for their lives than what they could have imagined. It not only changes his direction but changes him eternally and in his identification with God. Romans 1: 1 1 Paul, a servant of Jesus Christ, called to be an apostle and set apart for the gospel of God, - please notice he embraces God's plan for his life so strongly it is how he introduces himself. He is identified with Christ completely. The new Testament written mostly by the Apostle Paul shows his love for God; planted churches in most of the Middle East and Europe.

The Charismatic Movement

The 1970's was significant to born again spirit-filled Christians because there was a release of the Charisma of God – the gifts of the Holy Spirit – people in denominational churches started seeking God and getting baptized in the Holy Spirit. Christians began to move in the gifts of the spirit in their local churches. Tremendous healing Evangelists like Kathrine Kulman and Oral Roberts saw healings and miracles in their services. There was a tremendous move of the Spirit of God as people pressed in to know Him and serve Him.

Excellent Bible Teachers and preachers rose to fame and the fivefold ministry was almost in complete operation in the church (There were only some known Prophets and not many known Apostles to most of the Charismatic or Pentecostal Church.). I don't know what happened to the Charismatic Movement. Historically, we had a movement of Pastors teaching in the 1980's, Prophets in 1990's; and Apostles in 2000's, but I want the Charismatic in my life now. It is the person of God the Holy Spirit living in us– the gifts of God in operation through the people of God.

Local and Global

Believe God can reach you right where you are and use you. God will use you to build up the Body of Christ. (Ephesians 4) We are all called to encourage the Church, to build up and strengthen the parts of the Body of Christ we connect with. Each part of the Body helps to strengthen and encourage the people in your Church and in your Christian life. If there are ministries that bless you, you should also be praying for them, giving to them and volunteering for them if possible.

Freedom of Worship

Please remember that at this moment there are Christians being martyred because of their Christian faith. We should care for those members of the Body of Christ who do not have the freedoms we have in North America. Perhaps God will put on your heart to petition our government to stand up for those Christians' freedom. Perhaps you will start praying for them. We should be caring. We should be praying. We should be giving. We should care for them as though it was someone we knew and cherished deeply. Pray to ask God that you love His Church the way He loves His Church. Part of the traits of a Christian is that you love the Church – all Christians. You want to help them. You want freedom for them.

You are Not Alone

Don't ever believe the lie that you are alone. You are not alone. You are a member of the Body of Christ on the earth. There is not only a plan for your life concerning your vocation and family etc. but there is a Divine plan for you as a member His Church – that your live for the glory of God. There are Christians in your church who can pray with you and for you. There are Christians throughout the earth that can pray for you.

God will also use you to reach out to others making an eternal difference in their lives. You've got to be willing and you've got to be obedient. If you are truly seeking God and communing with Him, He will impart His will to you – He will share His heart – for people, animals, nations etc.

Spiritual Gifts and Natural Talents

Sometimes spiritual gifts and natural talents coincide. You might naturally be really good at music and God would use you in worship and praise. You might be good at sports and God could raise you up to be an athlete for Christ. Almost always they coincide. You will naturally like doing the things you are called to do.

Fruit of the Spirit

All the fruit of the spirit are important. Without the fruit – the gifts will be worth nothing. You are the planting of the LORD. You have gifts but also you want to grow in the fruit of the Spirit. Gal 5. Godly character traits and these fruit of the Spirit are essential so we show the love of Christ and minister with a pure heart. God wants us to be in the spirit, pure, holy. God could use angels. God could use animals. He wants to use you.

Knowing Your Spiritual Gifts

We have talked about the importance of knowing that you have spiritual gifts. It is possible, you could be a born-again spirit filled Christian and not know that you have spiritual gifts. Or you may not know what you are functioning in already is a spiritual gift. It is also possible that you might not use them should you have them, If you do not use your gifts, you will not develop in them or increase them.

Once you are baptized in the Holy Spirit, there should be a natural release of the giftings of the Holy Spirit in your life. If you have received the baptism in the Holy Spirit but are not praying in the Holy Spirit, you are not getting the benefits of praying in the spirit. Part of the benefits of praying in the Holy spirit – in tongues – is that you stir up your spiritual gifts and you are in the spirit realm. In the spirit is the only place you can grow and develop your spiritual gifts.

You are a spirit; you have a soul and you live in a physical body. I describe it this way: your spirit, before you are born again, is like a shriveled up balloon. Once you are born again – it is as though there is some air in the balloon but it isn't at its full potential. Once you are baptized in the Holy Spirit, it is like the Holy Spirit fills you so much – it is though the balloon is completely filled with helium and takes on a unique shape but also rises up high into the air. It is no longer bound by the limitations of things in the earthly realm. It has a new potential.

The Baptism of the Holy Spirit

The Baptism of the Holy Spirit is a gift in itself, but it is not for no reason. We use it because it is God's way of communicating with us surpassing or superseding our brain. I do mean it literally. God goes right to the spirit – to communicate with us as we are praying in the Holy Spirit. Often, if you continue to pray in tongues, He will translate it for you, not always, but almost always – so that your brain can understand it. What I am talking about is living in the spirit, becoming strong in the spirit so that you, the spiritual you, is stronger than the human will, mind or emotions, and stronger than your physical body.

You are living in a different realm – the high calling of God for your life – to live as a spiritual person, to live as a spiritual person. Soon after a person is baptized in the Holy Spirit, there should be some teaching on the gifts of the spirit. I'm not against teaching it before it occurs, but the person will benefit the most afterwards. If you do not know the gifts are there, you might not even know it is a gift. You could be already functioning in it, but without teaching, you may not know it is something you can grow in and use for God's glory.

For instance, I'll give you an example from scripture; Joseph who had dreams may not have known it was a gift from God. He spoke it so freely with his family; if he had known it was a special gift from God, he might have also prayed about it and asked God for wisdom concerning it. If you do not know, you should not; it's possible to share your most intimate revelations from God with those who will only laugh at you or hate you for it. God used images and visions to speak to him and give him prophetic insight as to what would happen in his life.

Your Gifts Are Precious

You should be taught to know your gifts and also to treasure them and only discuss them with people of like precious faith. It is something you want to keep, you want to use, you want to protect. I know of some people who take their best jewelry or most precious belongings and lock it up in a security box. The type of precious I am talking about here though is the type of precious we rely on every day such as H_2O. as precious as water or oxygen - something we completely rely on for our lives. It is fundamental to our operations. It is fundamental for us to know how to use our gifts, and be taught by those who can encourage us to use them.

Matthew 25 is along this serious note of recognizing your gift and using it. I'm not talking about a gift you received but wore or used once because it is not your favourite. You could put it on in front of company so they could see you wore it. That is a gift you show but don't regard as important. Something you use every day, something you don't want to live without.

Everyone has a favourite shirt or pair of shoes or something you want to use every day. The baptism of the Holy Spirit is also not only precious but He is essential to your success in finding your purpose in life and fulfilling it. The parable of the talents

Matthew 14: 14 "Again, the kingdom of heaven is like a man traveling into a far country, who called his own servants and entrusted his goods to them. 15 To one he gave five talents,[a] to another two, and to another one, to every man according to his ability. And immediately he took his journey. 16 He who had received the five talents went and traded with them and made another five talents. 17 So also, he who had received two gained another two. 18 But he who had received one went and dug in the ground and hid his master's money.

19 "After a long time the master of those servants came and settled accounts with them. 20 He who had received five talents came and brought the other five talents, saying, 'Master, you entrusted to me five talents. Look, I have gained five talents more.'

21 "His master said to him, 'Well done, you good and faithful servant. You have been faithful over a few things. I will make you ruler over many things. Enter the joy of your master.'

22 "He who had received two talents also came and said, 'Master, you entrusted me with two talents. See, I have gained two more talents besides them.'

23 "His master said to him, 'Well done, you good and faithful servant. You have been faithful over a few things. I will make you ruler over many things. Enter the joy of your master.'

24 "Then he who had received the one talent came and said, 'Master, I knew that you are a hard man, reaping where you did not sow, and gathering where you did not winnow. 25 So I was afraid, and went and hid your talent in the ground. Here you have what is yours.'

26 "His master answered, 'You wicked and slothful servant! You knew that I reap where I have not sown, and gather where I have not winnowed. 27 Then you ought to have given my money to the bankers, and at my coming I should have received what was my own with interest.

28 " 'So take the talent from him, and give it to him who has ten talents. 29 For to everyone who has will more be given, and he will have an abundance. But from him who has nothing, even what he has will be taken away.

Using the Talents

I want to bring the literal figures here. A person in authority gave the money to the different servants. They were precious assignments. They could have invested the money. They could have bought stuff with the money. They could have entered a business arrangement. They could have done something with the money to cause it to multiply or grow. They knew the person was going to come back for whatever was his. He had given them personal assignments. They were not given the same amount.

The one that had five, well he doubled his investment. He was faithful to use it so that is was multiplied. The one that had two, was faithful to use it to multiply it. The one who had one talent, he had a very negative image of his boss. He also confessed it to his boss. He said he knew the boss was hard and was taking things from places he didn`t sow. He is complaining about his task and he has a negative attitude. We don't know why he is negative. What he did, he did out of fear. He dug a hole and buried that talent. He thought only of giving back exactly what was given to him. His fear stopped him from trying to invest it or sow it or use it.

Encourage yourself to discover and use your gifts and talents

The more gifts and talents that you have, the more places you can use them for God's glory. Natural gifts and talents are important: music, education, art, sports, etc. those abilities you have should be developed. Someone should be encouraging you to develop them. The main person who could be encouraging you to develop them is you, partnering with the Holy Spirit. You should be encouraging your own self to use your talents and gifts for the glory of God. Do whatever you do with all you might and to the best of your ability to God.

If you're an artist, do it as unto the Lord. If you are an athlete, train and do your best. Aim to be the most Christ like player they have ever seen. Yes, it is a natural thing but you can glorify God in the natural. Even in the most mundane task, do it excellently. Your washing the dishes, do it the best possible way. You`re doing household chores, do them the best you can. You should be the person, within your own self motivating yourself to do your best; encourage your own self to do what you do as unto Christ.

In the talents parable, the one who had five, gained another five. I want you also to transfer it to spiritual gifts. What you use and do excellently will grow and God will shine through you.

The only way spiritual gifts can grow is by exercising them, using them. They grow by being used. God gives you wisdom and guidance as you use the gifts.

Exercising Your Gifts and Talents

Natural talents – Ask anyone who can play an instrument if he or she practices and truth is yes he or she practice. To keep sharp and precise, you practice – use it. I have known young people who are in the gifted range literally on a standardized test – genius potential in areas who waste their gifts. They do it because they don't have the right stimulus or won`t come under discipline, or submit to a teacher who can help them to grow in their gifts and talents. They could have attained the highest grades and career but they drop out of school – perhaps bored. Even if you are not one of these people, you always have something to give or use. The one with the five talents used them wisely. It is not the number of gifts and talents that makes the difference but your faithfulness to use them and multiply them. Please notice the way the boss spoke to them ``you are a faithful steward. `` Faithfulness is a key quality.

Discipline

Faithfulness has to do with practice, use and also I want to attach the art of discipline. This is self-discipline to do it but also discipline that you would learn from others who could help you to grow and give you wise council. You might call it mentorship. I would call it as an aspect of spiritual discipling or parenting. We should care about the other parts in the body of Christ. We should encourage them and teach them to train others. I`ve known several people who are very gifted musically. I have seen some selfish with their gift. This can be in any gifting. Being selfish, not caring about imparting the gift to others is an error. It can exist even in the body of Christ but it should not. I even believe it is a sin to be selfish with your gifts and not want to share it or impart it to others.

I have also seen others, like my friend with the musical gifts pouring into young people, training them in music and in the manor and attitude concerning using the gift wisely for God`s glory. There are spiritual parents – mentors in the body of Christ who can spot your gift and encourage you to use them. They are people who will care to invest of their lives into those who have potential but are not using it as excellently as they could. Having a mature friend to encourage you to use your gifts, and who can give you wisdom from experience related to it is special. This is a person who will invest his or her time, energy, effort and speak words of encouragement to you. Literally they sharpen you as iron sharpens iron to help you to be the best you can be. It cannot be forced. If you have to force people to care for each other, it is not the Body of Christ. It can`t simply be a program. It is God`s spirit that draws the people together for the mutual profit of both. There is joy in imparting to others.

Sow into others' lives

Part of your faithfulness in stewardship of your spiritual gifts is being able to sow into people's lives. Sow the knowledge and the things God has taught you about your gift into young people's hearts. Share the things you have learned by experience. Please let me encourage you to share; some people believe that experience is the only way to learn. It is true that experience can be a teacher but please also know you can learn from the wisdom of others who give their testimony. We can learn from others – we can avoid making the same mistakes they made.

Spiritual Mentors or Spiritual Parents

There are people who love God with all their heart and who also love you who will give you godly advice. They can help you to make decisions based on their truthful testimonies. You can learn from seasoned people. You can learn from Elders and deacons. Please don't think I mean the church title of Elder alone – I mean they are people who are functioning in that function. Hopefully, they are in positions of authority in the church. These are people who care about others and want to help them develop their gifts and talents. It doesn't have to be a cell group but it could take place in a cell group.

There should be people besides the pastors who sow into people's lives. There should be mature leaders who function under the authority of the pastor who teach, who lead small groups etc. Not every person has to attend every meeting at a local church. I am not talking about Sunday service; I am talking about each day of the week; different people could be gathering for different purposes at the local church. That's what makes us the Body of Christ. We care for each other. An active church that is healthy is a church that has all types of giftings operating in the church.

Invest; Don't Hoard

The giver is the opposite of that person in the parable with one talent. The giver is motivated by love. He or she invests and gives to people so they may grow spiritually. They invest their lives into others. It's not only about "me and my ministry". It is about developing others so they can grow in Christ. The one with the one talent is hoarding the one talent he has and won't share and doesn't invest. I believe that if you are selfish with your talents, you will reap what you sow.

If you are selfish in motive, only caring about your own self, you are not flowing in the Holy Spirit. There could be unclean things such as pride or covetousness – that are the root cause of your behavior. The good news is – Jesus can set you free. If you will repent, Jesus can wash you, fill you and use you for His glory. Part of the miracle – is that you will truly care for other members in the Body of Christ. Our new born-again nature is to be a giver – to be a helper – to care for others.

A Faithful Steward

Being faithful with your gift is a key to using it wisely. The ruler or boss, is not seen the same by the person with five talents. That person saw the boss in a positive way and had no fear of him. Therefore, he was able to function in the spirit. He gives his report with confidence. The one with one talent has a perverted or distorted view of his boss. Because of his fear and distorted view of his boss, he reacts in fear, burying his talent and gets no increase, and loses the one he talent he had.

Oh, if we could only learn to check the negative. A negative view or attitude must be cut off. We should pray to view others as Jesus does. Only the Holy Spirit in you can do it. He can immediately transform you so that the fear, and or root sins are gone from you in an instant and you are set free. Literally pray "Oh God, don't let me be negative. If I say something or thing something I shouldn't, correct me. And he will. The Holy Spirit will do it."

2 Corinthians 5: 10 For we must all appear before the judgment seat of

Christ, that each one may receive his recompense in the body, according to what he has done, whether it was good or bad. 11 Therefore, knowing the fear of the Lord, we persuade men. But we are revealed to God, and I trust we are also revealed in your consciences.

It says here we will give account for all things done in our bodies on earth. Every Christian will appear before the judgement seat of Christ. We will be judged as believers. To whom much is entrusted, much shall be required. We are going to give account before Christ for our words, our thoughts, our deeds, our choices: including good, bad or indifferent. Any sin we haven't repented of; we have to give account of. We should have no sins in our lives. We should repent immediately and receive the atonement of Jesus blood. It is essential that we keep right with God.

Keep Clean; Be Holy

Keep your heart right with God; plead the blood over yourself. Pray that you live strong. If you sin, repent. Jesus blood washes and cleanses you from all sin and unrighteousness. Keep offering yourself as a living sacrifice constantly. Immediately repent. Let nothing be between you and God. Some people believe the bad part of sin is that God finds out about it and is not pleased with you. That is not true. The horrible thing about sin is it puts a block between you and God.

As that boss or lord in Matthew gave the talents, God has given us gifts and talents knit right into the very core of our being. They are knit in your natural DNA and your spiritual DNA. You inherit from your natural parents, certain traits etc. In your spiritual DNA, you have inherited gifts and talents and promises of God. The purpose for which you were created is on the inside of you. The Holy Spirit can help you to understand yourself and to use you so you will be joyful and rejoicing in your life as well as affecting others for the kingdom of God.

What You can do

God has a purpose for you and a place for you to be fulfilled. Those gifts and talents are to give God glory by helping and ministering to other people. Get all the education and training certificates you can get in the areas that interest you the most. In our North American society, we have an awesome privilege of freedom to worship and praise God. This freedom is not in every country. Also, we have elementary and high school, paid for by our country. That is not in other countries. We should be using our privileges. There are loans and grants and bursaries to help people get a diploma or degree. Please know without higher education it is tough to find a good job that pays well. Believe me, it is worth it even if you must get a student loan. The jobs you can get with diplomas and degrees are awesome and will give you hope of getting out of poverty.

Education and training – If there is a coop placement, take it. If there is an opportunity for an apprenticeship, take it. Here in Ontario, our high school students must complete 40 hours of community service before they get their diploma. Actually, this is completely excellent as it helps them to develop work experience and sometimes the students complete their education and back to those places employed there. First, it gets them going outside of their own selves – caring about others, meeting new people etc. Secondly, It gives them job experience.

Unfinished Opportunities

If you had a chance to finish your diploma but didn't do it, or finish your degree but didn't do it – it will eliminate opportunities from your life. If you started a diploma or degree and didn't complete it, I am asking you to consider prayerfully doing it. It will open other opportunities for your life. The more diplomas, degrees, training, certificates, all types of learning that is on this earth – the more of them you have, will not only make opportunities for you but so that God can use you to help more people. We should be aiming to be excellent in all aspects of our life.

If you had an opportunity to help someone, but didn't, don't believe it will go unnoticed. God knows. He will hold you accountable. Remember the other parable in Matthew 25.

Matthew 25:
34 "Then the King will say to those at His right hand, 'Come, you blessed of My Father, inherit the kingdom prepared for you since the foundation of the world. 35 For I was hungry and you gave Me food, I was thirsty and you gave Me drink, I was a stranger and you took Me in. 36 I was naked and you clothed Me, I was sick and you visited Me, I was in prison and you came to Me.'

37 "Then the righteous will answer Him, 'Lord, when did we see You hungry and feed You, or thirsty and give You drink? 38 When did we see You a stranger and take You in, or naked and clothe You? 39 And when did we see You sick or in prison and come to You?'

40 "The King will answer, 'Truly I say to you, as you have done it for

one of the least of these brothers of Mine, you have done it for Me.'

God notices things we do and don't do. It may seem like no one is noticing but God notices. If you could have helped but didn't – it matters. It is so important a matter that we will give account at the Judgement seat of Christ. The routines of life are important: kindness towards each other, caring, giving of your efforts, giving of your time… if you can help someone who cannot repay you, God will reward you.

Developing Your Gifts

As fine motor skills as developed in a person, so are spiritual gifts developed as we use them – as we exercise them – using them under the umbrella of learning. You can learn by yourself, but it best to learn in a local body of Christ helping the other parts of the Body of Christ, It isn't learned from the pulpit ministry only. You can learn in Bible classes, in small groups etc. The small group is an excellent place to learn how to use your gifts for God's glory. It is a safe environment. The people could be corrected and not embarrassed. Most people would feel more comfortable in a small group setting using their gifts when they are first using them.

The training and equipping I received about spiritual gifts and ministry I count as so dear to me, so precious. They invested their lives into me. I thank God for them. I still love them and care for them, even those it is many years later. They were there to strengthen me, encourage me, and almost they do with a horse – placing a carrot out before the horse so that the horse would press on towards the goal- those people saw potential in me and encouraged me to press forwards into growing in Christ.

Their prodding for me to use my gifts and talents, was all in comfort and love. They kept saying – please use your gift. They kept encouraging me to pray for people, to lead worship, to lead people to Christ etc. They held me close to them so that I could learn from them. This is a sign someone has a true pastoral heart, he or she encourages you to use your gifts and talents. Instead of trying to hoard the people, they are trying to train up people and send them out to get people saved, healed, set free, needs met etc. We must care about the Body of Christ not only local but global. Developing our gifts and talents is essential for Christians so that we might train up and equip others.

***Please do the spiritual gifts survey in the next chapter. Record your top three scores. Prayerfully consider the chapters about your gifts and talents. Reading the other chapters will help you to understand others with different gifts.

2 MOTIVATIONAL GIFTS INVENTORY

On a Scale of 1 – 5 with 1 being low and 5 being high record your totals of the truth of these statements:

1. __Hypocrisy in yourself or others really bothers you.
2. __You help complete other people's projects before finishing your own.
3. __You speak all you know about a topic while having a conversation with someone.
4. __You have examples of people that God is growing? You use these personal examples while preaching or teaching or sharing with others.
5. __You are a good money manager and wise with money.
6. __If You are receiving or giving instructions, you want them very specific.
7. __You like to stay at home rather than be with large groups of people.
8. __You often make judgements quickly.
9. __You emphasize practical needs.
10. __You believe scriptural truth comes first, and that human experience is applied to that truth.
11. __You become impatient with a lack of progress in those you are helping.
12. __You give by logical need rather than emotional appeal.
13. __You like to organize people or groups.
14. __People who are not sensitive to others bother you.
15. __You speak sharp words.
16. __You are persistent – even pushy- if you know you are right.
17. __You focus on details so much you may lose sight of the bigger picture.
18. __You have to be careful about motivating others for personal gain.
19. __You always give to God\s work no matter how many bills you have to pay.
20. __Once you have established a goal you are persistent to achieve it.
21. __It is easy for you to get close to other people.
22. __You a confident speaker in front of groups.
23. __You genuinely, deeply care for others.
24. __ You enjoy learning, doing research and organizing facts
25. __ You waste time with people who are not interested in growing spiritually.
26. __You focus on meeting immediate material needs.
27. __You can choose clear objectives and not get stuck on the details.
28. __You are someone who can easily empathize with others.

29. __You are motivated to reveal unrighteous motives by presenting God's truth.
30. __You make personal sacrifices to meet the need of others.
31. __You would like to learn Hebrew or Greek so you could understand the Bible more.
32. __You enjoy setting courses of action to help others grow in their faith.
33. __You believe that God will prosper you so that you can give to others.
34. __You use people with gifts and talents to establish common goals.
35. __It is hard for you to be firm with others.
36. __You make quick judgements about people when you first meet them.
37. __You enjoy meeting needs that will free someone to do something else.
38. __You take notes in the services and read them afterwards.
39. __You enjoy encouraging others in their spiritual growth.
40. __You entrust finances and resources to others to further their ministry.
41. __People choose you to lead them in activities or situations.
42. __You can literally relate to a person so much you care to help him/her as much as possible?
43. __You categorize people into different kinds of groups.
44. __You like to help others whether or not you receive the credit for it.
45. __You are concerned about obtaining truth?
46. __You enjoy giving others advice.
47. __You genuinely care for needs of strangers.
48. __You focus on reaching the goal: goal oriented
49. __You rejoice when others rejoice, and weep with them who weep.
50. __You despise that which is evil.
51. __You are usually helping others.
52. __You enjoy research and in depth study.
53. __You are patient with those who are not quick to progress.
54. __If someone tells you of a physical need, you are able to make a quick decision of whether it is genuine.
55. __You like to lead or manage.
56. __You enjoy comforting those who are hurting.
57. __If you knew there were a particular sin in a congregation, you would feel you should confront them as a church?
58. __You have the ability to detect personal needs in others
59. __You enjoy researching and proving truth
60. __You prefer a one on one ministry approach.
61. __God has blessed you and prospered you so you can give to others.

62. __You like to organize and plan the activities of others to reach common goals.
63. __It easy for you to emphasize with others. (feel what they feel?)
64. __You would enjoy speaking to groups.
65. __You enjoy meeting practical needs of others.
66. __You prefer a study Bible more than other translations.
67. __You want to stimulate the faith of others.
68. __You have good business sense.
69. __It is easy to establish major objectives and help those around you to understand them.
70. __If a person is hurting, it is easy for you to relate to that person.

How to score the Motivational Gifts Inventory?

Place your number score next to each of the questions; add the totals:

Totals

Prophet=   1,__ 8,__ 15__, 22,__ 29,__ 36,__ 43,__ 50__, 57,__ 64__

Server =   2,__ 9,__ 16__, 23__, 30__, 37__, 44__, 51,__ 58__, 65__

Teacher =   3,__ 10,__ 17.__24, __31,__ 38__, 45,__ 52,__ 59,__

66__

Exhorter – 4,__ 11, __18,__ 25,__ 32,__ 39,__ 46,__ 53,__ 60,__ 67__

Giver -   5,__ 12,__ 19,__ 26,__ 33,__ 40,__ 47,__ 54,__ 61,__ 68.__

Ruler -   6,__ 13,__ 20,__ 27,__ 34,__ 41,__ 48,__ 55, __62,__ 69__

Mercy   7, __14, __21, __28, __35, __42,__ 49,__ 56,__ 63,__ 70__

Add up your totals for your gifts. Give your totals.

What are your predominant 3 or 4 gifts?

What are some characteristics about you that are a complete direct match with those gifts?

What Biblical characters you most identify with ? Why?

• With Reference to the Spiritual gifts Inventory from Bethesda Missionary Temple, Detroit, MI (Ann Beall 1981)

After you have completed the Inventory and have your top 3 or 4 motivational gifts, you may directly read about those gifts in the chapters that follow. They will give you traits, information on using them, Biblical examples, and hopefully encourage you to develop and use your spiritual gifts

I also highly recommend that you read the other motivational gifts to help you understand others in the body of Christ and why they do what they do. It will hopefully help us to help each other and strengthen each other as members of the Body of Christ.

3 MOTIVATION OF PROPHECY

The motivation of prophecy is often controversial. Throughout the Bible God's prophets were not always treated with respect. Prophets care about God's truth, care about conveying God's truth; they literally care about what God cares about. They usually have such a close relationship with God that they share God's heart and care about the things God cares about. It is similar to a close intimate friendship; you start caring about the things the other person cares about and you share that interest because of the other person. Prophets will usually pray God show me how to care about what you care about.

The Operation of the Gift

Prophets want to be friends of God. God has revealed Himself and His love for them and His people, that they want to show love towards God with their lives. They not only want to receive from God, but they also desire to give to God. God uses them to reveal righteous and unrighteous motives in people. God uses them in the gift of the spirit such as discerning of spirits and they are given information about things that only God knows. An example of this is in the New Testament when Nathaniel is coming speak with Jesus because it is the gathering of the LORD's disciples, Jesus declares "Here is an Israelite indeed, in whom is no guile." (John 1:47)

This means no bitterness, no hardness, a soft and tender, willing heart. Right after this Nathanael questions how he knows this. Jesus reveals righteous motives. It is not as though Jesus is talking with him finding out about him but it is the gift of discerning of spirits or it is an example of "reading the person's spirit".

Manifestation Gifts Often Associated

Prophets usually flow in the gifts of discerning of spirits, words of wisdom, words of knowledge. God uses them to see and declare what only God could know about someone to glorify God. Sometimes, it results in immediate repentance. There were some awesome prophets in this past century such as William Branham. He was a mighty man of God – but later went off track completely. During the glory of the LORD using him, he would literally see, as it were visions of the person he was praying for. He would be able to describe the vision he saw and sometimes people would begin weeping; sometimes people would be instantly healed as Brother Branham spoke the vision as God revealed it.

He operated in a tremendous anointing of the Holy Spirit; it was an open vision – that is the proper term for that type of prophecy. He described it as like seeing a movie of part of the person's life. You could get much excellent information from the God's Generals Series by Roberts Liardon. He has documented much important information about the leaders of the last century; there is a DVD series and also books.

WARNING – Stay in your Gifting

As you study a prophet's life, you will see that prophets don't always do everything right. Sometimes they screw up or sin, but we can still learn from the positive aspects of their lives. We can learn to do the right things and learn to stay away from the negative things by keeping ourselves from the same types of situations. Brother Branham became so popular and famous as a prophet that he did not have wise counsel. He was not well educated and he started to teach doctrine – without proper Biblical knowledge and got over into error and false doctrine. The people around him worshipped him so much – they went along with him rather than bring correction. Liardon notes a keen observation that had Branham stayed in only the prophetic and paired with a true Bible Teacher or preacher, most likely he would not have gotten into error.
The Bible is filled with people who didn't do everything right, but it doesn't mean we can't learn from them.

Motivated by Prophecy to Reveal Motives

If you were a prophet and you really only revealed righteous motives, you might not have much to say. That is my joke – the last statement but often it could be true. If you only prophesied favour and blessing and abundance prophecies over people, you would get many speaking engagements as a motivational speaker. Everybody like to hear positive things. Prophets are also motivated to expose wrong things, unrighteous motives, consequences of disobedience etc. This is where it is not so pleasant to be a prophet because God reveals truths and unpleasant consequences some of them that directly affect the prophet also.

An example of this would be in Jeremiah where God uses Jerimiah to speak to the King of Israel and warn him that he should surrender to the king of Babylon to avoid his own death and the murder of many people of Israel.

What happens is the king of Israel rejects it because he doesn't want to receive the truth that is enemy is going to overtake him and defeat Israel. Jeremiah was not speaking his opinion or personal advice. Jeremiah was speaking God's Word to the King. It was certainly what would occur with a hope for less casualties if the king obeyed. The King did not obey because he didn't understand that the prophet was speaking directly from God.

When Nebuchadnezzar of Babylon does come into the city and plunders it, and destroys it as it was prophesied, Nebuchadnezzar immediately sets Jeremiah free. All of Babylon had heard of the prophecies of Jeremiah and the king of Babylon gives Jeremiah a place of honour. He gives Jeremiah the choice of staying in Israel or going wherever he wants to go. He treats him with more respect than the king of Israel. It isn't because he is such a wise and God fearing person; I'm positive the fact the prophecies were for his own good were a factor in his treatment of Jeremiah. I don't believe he would have liked it as much if the prophecies were against him.

Communicate Truth

Prophets care about communicating the truth – even if it is not popular or what people want to hear. Prophets may seem to be harsh or judgmental if they are not tempered. What I mean by that is literally as with iron work, where a piece of molten hot metal is shaped by the tools of the blacksmith, so God matures and uses his prophets, strengthening them and developing Godly character and mercy in them. The prophet must learn to speak what God says and not add any words to it. The prophet must care for the people he or she is prophesying to.

A fleshly prophet, one living in his or her soul (mind, will emotions) and speaking prophecy with any other motive than to speak God's truth and reveal God's will, will not glorify God, The Prophet must be careful about guarding his/ her heart about loving people and praying for mercy even if he or she knows there is a judgement of God spoken. A true seasoned godly prophet will intercede for the people or persons he or she is prophesying over. The prophet must be led by the Holy Spirit not any selfish motive. A mature prophet will guard his or her words carefully.

The Tongue

Guarding the mouth is something all of us as Christians must learn. If you read the book of James, it tells us to guard our words. Proverbs informs us that we can speak life or death with our mouths. Even though the tongue is small in the body, the effects of the words we speak can be significant. I would highly recommend that with all spiritual gifts, we learn about the truths of guarding our words.

If you have spoken words and wish you had not spoken them, you can never get them back. You should pray for God's forgiveness and mercy concerning any of these instances. There have been excellent teaching on this topic within the last several years: Charles Capps, Kenneth Hagin, Kenneth Copeland, Joyce Meyer to name a few. If you have not heard any teaching on this topic of guarding the words you speak and you are serious about doing something for God, I recommend you study the mouth and the effects of words: about ourselves, towards others, in prayer etc.

Don't Add to God's Word

If you have ever been hurt by someone's words, you know what I'm saying. A teacher for instance can encourage or discourage a student by the words spoken. A prophet person, speaking with an unction by God, carrying the heart of God, should speak with wisdom and exactness, avoiding personal opinion or feeling. This is an area of warning to the prophetically motivated but also to all those with spiritual gifts.

Motivated by Love

I also want to emphasize that all the gifts flow through love. The fruit of love, a heart loving with the love of Christ – that Agape love – should be our primary motivation for ministry and should be the fruit evidenced in our using of the gifts. Jesus is love. Our God is love. If we are truly are flowing with the spirit of God, love will be evident. The apostle Paul speaks to us:

Ephesians 4: 15 But, speaking the truth in love, we may grow up in all things into Him, who is the head, Christ Himself,

If our gifts are not flowing through the fruit of love, the character of Christ, they will be ineffective.

1 Corninthians13 If I speak with the tongues of men and of angels, and have not love, I have become as sounding brass or a clanging cymbal. 2 If I have the gift of prophecy, and understand all mysteries and all knowledge, and if I have all faith, so that I could remove mountains, and have not love, I am nothing.

Jesus Himself spoke judgements; he even got angry. Jesus words to the Pharisees and Sadducees and those who tried to stop people from believing in Him or getting to know the truth seem very harsh but they were not fleshly words. They were God's words. His anger was righteous indignation. He was speaking God's words to those who oppose God Himself.
Matthew 23: 13 "Woe to you, scribes and Pharisees, hypocrites! You shut the kingdom of heaven against men. For you neither enter yourselves, nor allow those who are entering to go in. 14 Woe to you, scribes and Pharisees, hypocrites! You devour widows' houses and for pretense make long prayers. Therefore, you will receive the greater condemnation.

15 "Woe to you, scribes and Pharisees, hypocrites! You travel sea and land to make one proselyte, and when he becomes one, you make him twice as much a son of hell as yourselves.

Jesus' motives were first love for God and secondarily love for people. Someone prophetically motivated should not have a selfish desire to "go tell people all their faults". That is not a motivation from God. That is a critical spirit and a fleshly person. God only reveals someone's sins or negative aspects if God is softening that person's heart to repent. A person who is overly critical is not a person motivated by love.

Prophets Care About God's Truth

The prophet must function as a part of the body of Christ with the other members of the Body of Christ – with love flowing through us. It is hard for a prophet to notice something that isn't right in the local church. If a prophet sees something that is not in line with scripture or honouring to God, that prophet will speak against it. He or she will immediately want to correct it – with a strong desire. In a church service, the Pastor presiding should give the correction. The correct channel or direction would be for the prophet to give the word to the pastor and let that person bring the correction.

In the Old Testament we see examples of prophets who pronounced judgements against corrupt kings or corrupt people; this was not received well and most prophets were martyred. An example similar in the New Testament is the first martyr Stephan. He was prophetically correcting those who spoke against Jesus. He reviewed all of God's history with Israel and Jesus' fulfillment of Messianic prophecy and speaks these strong but true words:

Acts 7: 51 "You stiff-necked people, uncircumcised in heart and ears! You always resist the Holy Spirit. As your fathers did, so do you. 52 Which of the prophets have your fathers not persecuted? They have even killed those who foretold the coming of the Righteous One, of whom you have now become the betrayers and murderers, 53 who have received the law by the disposition of angels, but have not kept it."

The people did not repent. Their hearts were hardened even more and they stoned Stephan to death. At some point a prophet will come into contact with someone that does not care about God's heart. Stephan says the biggest insult possible to the Pharisees by calling them uncircumcised in heart. They practiced physical circumcision as a physical sign they were God's chosen people. He is insulting them saying their hearts are uncircumcised or pagan. It is hard to believe they got so angry until you know what it means. He blames them for the murder of Jesus and the prophets.

Stephan is speaking in severe language that I would term "righteous rage". He is speaking God's word but it is with the anger of God towards those who have continually rejected him. This outpouring of righteous rage – directly leads to Stephan's death,

Righteous rage from a prophet can lead the people in two responses. They can immediately repent and be forgiven, or they can harden their hearts and reject God again.an example of this where the results are different is in the instance of Nathan the prophet confronting king David on his sin.

1 Samuel 12: 7 Then Nathan told David, "You are this man! Thus says the Lord, the God of Israel: I anointed you as king over Israel and I rescued you from the hand of Saul. 8 I gave to you your master's house and your master's wives into your arms, and I gave to you the house of Israel and Judah. If this were too little, I would have continued to do for you much more. 9 Why have you despised the word of the Lord by doing evil in His sight? You struck down Uriah the Hittite with the sword, and you took his wife as a wife for yourself. You killed him with the sword of the Ammonites. 10 Now the sword will never depart from your house, because you have despised Me and have taken the wife of Uriah the Hittite to be your wife.
11 "Thus says the Lord: See, I will raise up trouble against you from within your own house. I will take your wives before your eyes and will give them to your neighbor, and he will lie with your wives in broad daylight. 12 Although you did it secretly, I will do this thing before all of Israel, and

under the sun."

In this passage. Nathan directly points the finger at David and tells his sin. King David didn't know anyone knew. He tried to keep it a secret, but God knew. His response is totally different. When confronted with His sin, David repents. "13 Then David said to Nathan, "I have sinned against the Lord.""

Prophetic Preaching

Notice that because David repents, the severity of the judgement is lessened. It is still horrible and severe, but there is mercy given as David's heart was truly repentant. He gets his life and he keeps his kingdom. That is amazing. Righteous rage will reveal the heart attitude of the person. The person will repent or become hard hearted. A prophet who preaches brings such a conviction with his or her preaching that often congregations fall to their knees in repentance or in the awesome presence of God that accompanies the preaching.

The Apostle Peter also has a similar word to Stephan as he preaches on the day of Pentecost. The 120 who were praying in the upper room and received the baptism of the Holy Spirit, were compelled to go into the streets where they were prophesying and speaking in other tongues they had not learned. The Spirit of God was on them very much. Some ignorant people accused them of being drunk, The Apostle Peter is enraged at this. He preaches the Messianic scriptures to the point of Jesus death and resurrection. He speaks words of judgement.

Acts 2: 36 "Therefore, let all the house of Israel assuredly know that God has made this Jesus, whom you have crucified, both Lord and Christ."

The people immediately reacted. They asked how they might be saved. Peter gives them a word of encouragement. He tells them to repent and be baptized. Over 2,000 people came to Christ that day. The people who were there were pilgrims coming from other nations to worship at Pentecost. They heard with spiritual ears, desiring to know God. Their hearts were softened by the words of righteous rage. They repented and accepted Jesus. The early Church grew from 120 to over 2, 000 people in one day because of his prophetic preaching.

If You Are Not Sure – Wait

If you are motivated by the gift of prophesy and you are not sure if you should say something or not – don't. Pray and wait until you are sure. If it is something negative especially – don't say it unless you know that it is God speaking. If you are in a church – submit yourself to the presiding pastor. You could share that word with him or her and leave it up to him or her to speak it to the congregation. God gives pastors a special anointing to care for their sheep. They are protective of their sheep but they will speak a word of correction if they believe it is God's word. You could write it out and give it to your pastor. The pastor would use his or her discernment to give the word. Come under authority of the leader in that place.

Need for Prophets

There isn't always a prophet in the ministry team at a church. It is so important that prophets and pastors etc. communicate and have good relationships. God wants all the five-fold ministry in the church: Apostles, prophets, evangelists, teachers, pastors. We must have the gift of prophecy in our churches or this is a negative thing.

God uses all the gifts of the spirit to build up the church. Prophetic motivation is necessary as are all the gifts. They help to build up, establish, strengthen and keep the local church. We've got to be able to flow together as a body. So if someone in the congregation has given you a message that the LORD has spoken to him or her, don't reject it quickly. Be prayerful about it; you are accountable to God for the message. If the person is submitting himself or herself to you, use your authority with wisdom. If the prophet gives it to you, and you do not give it, you are responsible to give account to the LORD.

Beware of Harsh Tone

A word of direction to those motivated by prophesy, if it seems too harsh, it probably is too harsh. There are judgements. Many people will say "not in the new testament". Read about Ananias and Sapphira (Acts 5). Because these people on purpose lied to the Holy Spirit to a man of God, they died instantly and were taken out and buried. After their deaths, many people feared.

In a congregation, any prophetic word that comes forth, we should pray about and consider. We should have prophets teaching younger prophets.

1 Corinthians 14: 32 The spirits of the prophets are subject to the prophets.

It doesn't mean they don't submit to the pastors or leaders of the local church. It means that they should be trained and apprenticed by elder prophets. What I am presently speaking about is speech. There are different types of prophecy. Most prophecy in the local church is edification, exhortation and comfort (1 Corinthians 14: 3).

Edification – building up strengthening
Exhortation – encouraging
Comfort – the comfort of God's peace

There could be Judgement or Correction

There are some New Testament Christians who believe that is all there is but sometimes there is judgement or correction. There are places where correction is given to congregations. The Apostle Paul is known for this. The Apostle Paul is famous for this with the Corinthian Church and even to the Apostle Peter.

Galatians 2: 11 But when Peter came to Antioch, I withstood him face to face, because he stood condemned. 12 Before certain men came from James, he ate with the Gentiles. But when they came, he withdrew and separated himself, fearing those who were of the circumcision.

Both the Apostle Paul and the Apostle Peter were being used by God to preach to the Gentiles (pagans – non Jews) and win them to Christ; Peter was mostly preaching to Jews but was at Antioch with Paul and eating and drinking with the Gentile converts – the early Christians. They were not following the Levitical Laws or teachings of Moses concerning food. Peter was enjoying himself with them until the Jews from Jerusalem came; he started to keep all the Jewish dietary rules after they came. Peter had been specifically been given a vision by God about the matter. God showed him a huge blanket with all sorts of unclean animals on it – things forbidden by the laws of Moses.

Acts 10: 15 The voice spoke to him a second time: "What God has cleansed, do not call common." 16 This happened three times. And again the vessel was taken up into heaven.

Peter was specifically used by God to lead Cornelius and his household to Jesus directly after this vision. They were all baptized in the Holy Spirit and then water baptized. This vision was used by God to reveal to Peter that God cared about the Gentiles and that the gift of salvation was for all people. Peter should not have pretended to be following all the laws of Moses for fear of what the Jews would say. It was an insult to the Gentile believers he had been with. Because of it, Paul corrected Peter. Do you know how much that mattered? That early Christians were so thankful to receive the Word of God from those who actually knew Jesus (Peter the disciple) that the insult against them was huge.

Communication with God

Prophets see things. Prophets dream dreams. God speaks to his prophets. God often speaks to prophets in symbols – things the prophet understands. Prophets have an aspect of their life that is directly supernatural. God communicates with them and speaks to them and through them. Prophets are called to intercessory prayer very strong: praying for their nation, praying for their church, praying for others; they intercede prophetically on behalf of people. They feel a strong compelling to pray.

Agabus

This prophet is not usually mentioned much but please notice, he gave a word to the apostle Paul. It was not exhortation, edification or comfort. It was a word of warning over Paul. He also demonstrates it by acting it out. The prophet is motivated to Prophecy in these ways: Speech is one aspect; demonstrating is the other. The prophet Agabus literally wraps the girdle around his hands and feet to symbolize what would happen to Paul.

Acts 21: 10 While we stayed there many days, a prophet named Agabus came down from Judea. 11 When he had arrived, he took Paul's belt and bound his own hands and feet, saying, "The Holy Spirit says, 'In this manner the Jews at Jerusalem shall bind the man who owns this belt and deliver him into the hands of the Gentiles.'"

Prophetic Actions or Demonstrations

In Exodus 7, Moses goes before Pharaoh with his staff, his walking stick that he had used to head sheep. One of the demonstrations that God told Moses to do was to throw down his stick so that it would become a serpent. Moses obeys; he throws it down and it becomes a serpent; God tells him to pick it up by the tail; Moses picks it up and it becomes a rod again.

Pharaoh's magicians had some magic and could duplicate the demonstration. However, Moses' serpent rod swallowed up all of the magicians of Egypt's rods. This is a demonstration. It is not for nothing. God uses it as a symbol of what He is going to do in Egypt. Often, the ruler of a nation would have a scepter in his hand and with it as a symbol of his power, he ruled the land. What is shown in this demonstration is a prophetic act in itself as what happens with Moses and Israel is that Jehovah God (I AM that I AM) totally defeats Egypt and Israel is set free because of it.

An example of prophetic demonstration also, can be seen with the prophet Ezekiel in passage below.

Ezekiel 4: 11 You also shall drink water by measure, the sixth part of a hin.[b] From time to time you shall drink it. 12 You shall eat it as barley cake, having baked it in their sight with dung that comes out of man. 13 Then the Lord said, "Even so the sons of Israel shall eat their defiled bread among the nations where I drive them."

Here God instructs the prophet to lay on one side of his body for so many days and to cook his food using human dung as a symbol. The prophet begs God for mercy because it is completely unclean and filthy. God does give him mercy and allows him to use cow dung instead. This was still considered completely unclean. God used the prophet to live out the representation of God's dealing with Israel. The actions of the prophet were considered by all who saw him. They paid attention because they knew it meant something. These prophet was living as holy as he could and such a thing was utterly repulsive to him.

A prophet will be motivated to speak but also to live it out. Often parts of their lives will be used to demonstrate to the people something God wants to communicate.

Moses, his life spared as a baby, to be raised in Pharaoh's home, who would be given the best education and training was an example to the people of God delivering Israel out of Egypt. Moses life was spared as a symbol of all of Israel that was delivered out of Egypt. They were born in slavery but they were brought out into freedom.
Pray for insight to the Scriptures

As you are reading your Bible, begin to pray asking God to show you demonstrations of the motivation of prophecy and people God used. Ask God to reveal the truths of scripture to you so you can impart to others. A good method is to pray "God show me" and God will bring it to you. The Holy Spirit is our teacher. He can bring scriptures to our remembrance, to teach us, enlighten us and give us wisdom. Pray asking the Holy Spirit to teach you and after He has done it, don't forget to thank Him for it. Say Thank You Holy Spirit.

Intercessory Prophet

The motivation of prophecy is often directly linked to strong intercessory prayer. The prophets throughout scripture would go off by themselves for days praying by themselves. John the Baptist was born into the priesthood, but went out into the wilderness, praying, prophesying. He would teach and prophesy to the people, but he would always go off by himself.

Jesus Christ Himself is our example in this. He taught the people and wherever he went people followed him but he also went off by himself to pray. Prophets will always go be alone with God; part of their calling is direct intimacy with God. That mostly happens when they are apart from the others. They usually not only pray for themselves but also they intercede for people often heir nation.

One of the most heartfelt prayers is Jesus praying over the city of Jerusalem. In Matthew 23, He not only sees the Jerusalem present but sees what is to come to the people He loves. He is crying and weeping as He prays.

Matthew 23: 37 "O Jerusalem, Jerusalem, you who kill the prophets and stone those who are sent to you, how often I would have gathered your children together as a hen gathers her chicks under her wings, but you would not! 38 Look, your house is left to you desolate. 39 For I tell you, you shall not see Me again until you say, 'Blessed is He who comes in the name of the Lord.'[a]"

Daniel and his friends became captives in Babylon. They also were given special honour as advisors to the king. He is praying for his people and begging for mercy. He is interceding for Jerusalem and for Israel as though it were for his own self. He is asking forgiveness for his sins and iniquities – he has not committed these things – he is directly identifying with the people he is praying for. He believes his people are his people just as much as he believes God is God.

Daniel 9: 17 "Now therefore, O God, hear the prayer of Your servant and his supplications, and for Your sake, O Lord, cause Your face to shine upon Your sanctuary, which is desolate. 18 O my God, incline Your ear and hear. Open Your eyes and look at our desolations and the city which is called by Your name, for we do not present our supplications before You for our righteousness, but for Your great mercies. 19 O Lord, hear! O Lord, forgive! O Lord, listen and act! Do not defer, for Your own sake, O my God. For Your city and Your people are called by Your name."

He cares about God's good name. He prays for mercy. He knows we, God's people, deserve wrath, but he prays for mercy.

In Exodus, after God had delivered Israel out of Egypt and brought her to Mount Sinai, Israel made a pagan altar and worshipped it as God while Moses was on the mountain speaking to God. God states He will completely destroy Israel. After Moses own fit of anger at Israel, he realizes he must intercede for Israel. Yes, they deserve wrath and judgement but Moses is interceding – praying for them as though for himself.

Moses is pleading for Israel. He reminds God of how He loved Israel and delivered her out of bondage. He reminds God of the covenants He made with Abraham, Isaac and Jacob. He quotes God to God. A prophet will pray and intercede for God's people, quoting God's Word to God asking for mercy. In fact, in some places God says to God" If you won't go with us, I won't go." Or "If you are going to kill them, kill me". He also cares about God's good name (vs 12) He reminds God of His plan to save Israel and begs for mercy identifying with Israel as an intercessor.

Exodus 32: 11 But Moses sought the favor of the Lord his God, and said, "Lord, why does Your wrath burn against Your people, whom You have brought forth from the land of Egypt with great power and with a mighty hand? 12 Why should the Egyptians speak, saying, 'With evil intent He brought them out, to kill them in the mountains and to destroy them from the face of the earth'? Turn from Your fierce wrath and relent of this harm against Your people. 13 Remember Abraham, Isaac, and Israel, Your servants, to whom You swore by Yourself, and said to them, 'I will multiply your descendants as the stars of the heavens, and all this land that I have spoken of will I give to your descendants, and they will inherit it forever.' "

14 Then the Lord relented of the harm which He said He would do to His people.

Prophets of God care about honouring God and His Word; they care about God's promises to His people; they care about God's reputation and O they love God's people. They stand in the gap, literally they pray and they intercede and ask God for mercy. They care for God's people.

A person motivated by prophetic gifting must keep pure. Let no bitterness, no anger, no unforgiveness, enter in. They should keep Jesus as the standard for righteousness on the earth. They should speak the truth in love, with mercy, with godly character, humility, coming into obedience with church authority. They should pray for God to give them mercy and compassion so they will pray for the people they are with. They should serve with genuine love doing what they do for the glory of God.

4 THE MOTIVATION OF SERVING

The gift of serving, actually exists in the Old Testament, before we recognize it in its modern form. In the new testament the term Deacon comes really from the Greek word diakonia which means to serve or help. It literally means someone who will meet practical needs. I am talking about very practical needs such as preparing a dinner, setting the tables, place settings, food preparation, washing the dishes, stacking chairs or being ushers in the church. The ministry of helps, we often see these people with the gift of serving raising their hands to help in any practical type of serving.

Practical Ways

Servants like to help in practical ways. This includes, passing out pamphlets or bulletins. These people are the first recruits of a pastor asks for volunteers to do something practical in the church. If they believe they can help in some practical way, they rejoice, take joy in doing it. They actually are motivated spiritual to lend a hand, to serve to give of their efforts, often releasing others to pursue the LORD in some way such as a service or Christian event, or even to release a single mother to attend a service.

The Motive

The Servant actually receives joy from serving someone else. People who do not have this motivation would not understand at all why these people do what they do. Some people would question their motives with the question, "What are they doing this for?" They may suspect some other motive because it is hard for them to understand what motivates a servant. Servants don't do it for money – even though they could end up in the service industry because they show excellence in all service skills. They don't do it for recognition although they are often noted for their excellence in service.

Their motivation is not praise from people although they like to be thanked or valued because what they are giving is of their very lives – their time, their efforts etc. If the servants have given their best but they are insulted because of it or not appreciated, they may grow a rough spot – a hardness of heart – like Martha of Bethany who complained that she was doing all the work and her sister was sitting at Jesus' feet (implying she was not helping). Usually. A true servant is humble about it; they do not seek recognition in public.

Their main motive is to serve with the motive of serving the LORD Jesus Christ.

They literally believe that if they serve people on earth, it is actually like serving the LORD Jesus Christ. They take literally Jesus' words on the following:

Matthew 25: 34 "Then the King will say to those at His right hand, 'Come, you blessed of My Father, inherit the kingdom prepared for you since the foundation of the world. 35 For I was hungry and you gave Me food, I was thirsty and you gave Me drink, I was a stranger and you took Me in. 36 I was naked and you clothed Me, I was sick and you visited Me, I was in prison and you came to Me.'

37 "Then the righteous will answer Him, 'Lord, when did we see You hungry and feed You, or thirsty and give You drink? 38 When did we see You a stranger and take You in, or naked and clothe You? 39 And when did we see You sick or in prison and come to You?'

40 "The King will answer, 'Truly I say to you, as you have done it for one of the least of these brothers of Mine, you have done it for Me.'

Literally they believe that serving people and caring for people is caring for Christ. At best, they do it with excellence and diligence, giving their best as though giving to Jesus Himself. The true servant knows that even if it seems insignificant, such as helping someone to carry parcels, or offering to care for a child, the LORD cares and he or she becomes the hands of Christ. God shares Hos love of people and the mundane aspects of life as being important to God because they are important to us.

Serving as unto Christ

Servants use serving people as serving Jesus Christ as their main motivation. Their deep love for people is genuine and spiritual. It may not seem spiritual but the origin is the Holy Spirit that prompts these people to give. Their motivation is in serving God by serving people. People who question their motives may think they are trying to earn favour for some other reason. The truth is they literally feel a prompting of the Holy Spirit to help those people.

Sometimes these people, because what they are doing is practical, may even doubt that what they are doing is spiritual. For example, let me give you an instance of my own mother. She would often get a feeling; it would be strongly impressed upon her spirit, that she should make extra food for dinner that day. She would make more than a normal amount of spaghetti or chicken or whatever: some to give to our neighbour (a single mum). Almost always we received tremendous thanks from her. It might have been the only supper they could have had that day. My mum would literally believe she should care for others and serve and give to them.

Other people would literally say "I should go over to help this person because I know he or she is doing some labour at home, such as painting or digging or such a task. They may offer to make dinner for them, help them in the task, watch the children, or help clean up afterwards. This may seem unimportant or insignificant to those who do not understand this gift.

God needs people who will serve in practical ways as well as those who minster the Word in preaching and teaching Christ. There is a large part of the Body of Christ called to minster as servants because there is a need for many helpers or servants. They serve in practical ways, assisting the other parts of the Body of Christ so they can function at their optimum level. Literally, they do things such as cook, bake, clean, paint, fix things, mow lawns etc. What is done by the servant to help the person, might be the only way that person could be able to do the rest of the project. It might be the encouragement that person needs – knowing that God is sending helpers to help him or her.

Levels of Gifting

There is a level of the gift, where people literally volunteer within the church when a request is made for helpers. But there is also a supernatural function of this gift. Those who use this gift will often get a strong feeling or impression to assist somebody to do a practical thing. Example, a person will strongly feel or think " I should go mow that person's lawn."

The Holy Spirit leads

That person will feel a strong recurring feeling that this is a priority – it is the Holy Spirit – impressing that person to serve in a practical way – sometimes as a direct answer to prayer by the person that needs the help. The person will offer this gift of service in obedience to the Holy Spirit. This is the supernatural ministry of the gift of serving. It is receiving and obeying direction from God.

It could be something like "I really feel I need to watch your children today. The two of you go and do something together." In this way, it could be a word of knowledge that the person actually needed to do something together to keep in spiritual harmony.

Misunderstood

Sometimes this gift is misunderstood. People ignorant of the gift or not sensitive to the Holy Spirit might think that it is only a physical thing the person is doing and not understand it is a spiritual blessing. They do not respect it as a spiritual gift. It is literally a spiritual blessing with one part of the Body of Christ coming to help the other parts.

The body helps itself

If you are nailing some wood and mistakenly hit your thumb, you may immediately suck on that thumb to try to numb the pain. Your body will react to help the part in need. You care for the parts of your body. If there is any pain, your hands might go to the spot to try to relieve it. This is an autonomic reflex – the body tries to preserve itself.

Just as the human body cares for itself, so should the Body of Christ care for itself.

Here is a very specific instance of it, very spiritual and very practical both. There was a person who had a death in his family and had to move out of the home he was in. It was atrocious. There was clutter, hoarding, uncleanliness, a horrible mess that was overwhelming for this young person to deal with. It was the result of ignorance, an ill elderly parent, and years of neglect. He did not have much money so he couldn't have paid for help. He had no other family so we the Church were his only family.

In this instance, the guy had to move, he could no longer live there, but he could not leave the mess. It seemed overwhelming to him. All it takes to get it started is one spiritual friend. That friend informed other people in our young people's group. She had motivation to serve and leadership ability. She gathered a team of people who literally went and helped clean out the garbage and pack what was valuable. My point here is the Pastor did not know of it or order the people to help. Parts of the Body of Christ came together to help complete the task. It was a supernatural natural response from the body of Christ in an important place in that young man's life. We were the only family he had.

The Body Should Help Itself

True Christian friends don't talk about the negative aspects to gossip. Instead they gather together to solve the issue. They pray about it but they don't pray about it out loud in public to be announcing it to anyone. Some stuff should be cared for by the Body of Christ as a direct response to a need. The Pastor doesn't have to be concerned about things that are easy for us to solve. I'm not talking about not respecting the pastor, I am saying the rest of the Body of Christ can serve and care for other parts of the Body of Christ.

Service to help someone should be our response as the Body of Christ. Pastors have so many other things they must care about; if we the Body of Christ would respond to a need. we could free the other members of the Body of Christ such as pastors, elders and deacons to minister to the needy.

The Body Serving

A second example I can give you, organized by an elder knew some people were moving and asked members of our cell group to volunteer to paint, to cook meals, to help physically move that couple and their children. I believe everyone in our cell group attending. The painting was done in a day. Men and women helped. Some people of the group prepared lunch and supper for us. We did not want anything; we were not in it for any other reason than to serve, bless and care for a family in our group.

That last example, I mentioned was at a Church I attended that was really high in servant ministry. People volunteered to mow lawns for those who needed help; there was a group of men from the church who decided to get together and help the single mothers and widows with practical tasks around the home. Things needed to be repaired; they did it; they were skilled in carpentry, plumbing etc. That is pretty amazing that it exists. Parts of the Body of Christ coming together to help other parts of the Body of Christ – demonstrating the true love of Christ by serving.

Those men saw the need. I believe God used them to spot the need. Those men volunteered of their time. They had families and commitments also. They saw the needs of others and knew that they together could solve these needs by joining together. They decided to honour the LORD in this way. In that Church we did not pay for cleaning staff. People took turns cleaning. I mean literally dusting, vacuuming, taking out the trash etc. And occasionally there was a day long gathering together to care for the church building and property.

Serve Within the Church Family

Even if you are a born again spirit filled Christian, you may not know that a person motivated to serve will spiritually serve God by giving of their efforts in ordinary ways. First, we should care for those in our own house. What I mean by that is we should serve those within our church family first. I wouldn't stop it there though.

Servant Evangelism

There is a denomination, one I have high regards for but am not a member of, the Vineyard, who literally use servant evangelism to win people to Christ. What they will do is buy coolers of ice water and bring them to large public events in blistering heat. They will give the water free to people with a kind word such as "Please receive this in the name of the Lord Jesus Christ. If there is anything we can do as a Church to help you, please contact us."

They also hold free car washes for the public. Their youth group will wash your car and share the love of Christ – offering spiritual refreshment such as "Please contact us if we can help you in any way." They use it as a method of evangelism. It is completely practical. Some people may think it is not spiritual what they are doing. In our economy, in our age of capitalism and desire for money and increase, people doing something for nothing is almost completely not heard of. Because of their service they are noticed by others. It stands out because it is different than what others do.

Why We Serve

Our Servant image will set us apart from the world. People will begin to talk about us and say – they must be Christians because they are serving for free. There they are serving for nothing. Do you get those people? They might laugh at us. They might even take advantage of our serving, but if we persist, we will win them by our love.

Yes, people may take advantage – for example, Christians sometimes offer Christmas or Easter Dinners for those who have no other place to go. People may pretend to be poor to get the free food. Yes, the servant is sometimes taken advantage of. Sometimes, the servant is so busy helping people he or she neglects his or her own needs at home. That is an extreme example. It is terrible that they are taken advantage of, but what would be worse is if servants didn't give, but they could have given and somebody who had a real need is neglected and alone rather than receiving a blessing from the Body of Christ. What if you mad a chance to be a blessing to a person but missed it? The true servant motivated by love of Christ would not be able to live with himself or herself.

Doing the Natural to Free Them for the Spiritual

Especially servants like to free up people from a natural task such as babysitting, so they can go to church or to a spiritual event. I know people who would offer to mow their pastor's lawn so their pastor can minister or be freed for prayer etc. I'm not talking about trying to win points with the pastor here. I am talking about caring that the pastor is able to minister, have refreshing etc. Often, pastors are pulled in so many directs with people who have needs who want something. The person who volunteers to help the pastor with genuine serving, cares for the Pastor as a part of the Body of Christ helping the other parts.

Honour Those Who Teach the Word

I have witnessed all sorts of treatments of pastors. Certainly there are extremes in it but I want to talk about caring for the pastor as important because often he or she is not considered as part of the Body. The truth is pastors need the gifts of the spirit in the members of the church operating; it encourages the pastor to be his or her best.

I have known people who would literally cook dinner for the pastors. One woman wanted them to have a nutritious, excellent lunch. She wanted nothing from them. She cooked it and brought it to them daily as unto God in service. The truth is the couple of pastors we had would either neglect to eat regular, pay for lunch nearby or eat unhealthy. She was a blessing to them. She did this for more than a year while she was trying to find a job. I believe her honouring the pastors literally blessed her with favour to get the awesome job she got.

The Motive Matters

Cooking can be serving; it depends why you are doing it and who you are doing it for. Do you desire to bless somebody with all your being so he or she has an excellent meal that that person might not get if you didn't give? That is serving through cooking. In the churches I have attended, if there was a need for food at a wedding or a funeral, the church covered it. I mean literally – people volunteered to cook the food, serve the food and clean up afterwards.

Why Serve?

Are you doing it to bless that person? That's a good reason. Are you doing it as unto the LORD? That is the best reason. You know who usually does this for us? Our mom and sometimes our dads, especially single dads. They cook for us, clean our clothes etc. Special love is released as they give of their lives to us. That same love is released as we give to parts of the Body of Christ who have a need.

Mechanics for Christ

I have known several Christian mechanics who made a good living, were doing well and busy but they also had a gift of serving and they would volunteer to fix someone in the church's car or truck for the price of parts alone. I have received of this special blessing particularly while I was on a tight budget as a student. I really had no way to get the car fixed unless someone helped me. God released those special men into my life who wanted nothing from me. I paid for the parts themselves.

Those men volunteered to repair the car. They believed they were doing God's will by blessing their brothers and sisters. The truth was correct. If they did not help me, I don't know what I would have done. Please know I was not the only one. These men helped many people in a similar way – using their trade and skill to serve the Body of Christ.

Many Servants

Serving ministry is a large proportion of the Body of Christ because we need practical help. There are different modes of serving. Some will serve in the nursery. Some will serve in the kitchen. Some will serve as ushers or cleaners. There will be those who serve primarily in church and those who serve in church and outside the church.

Serving is a strong motivation in the Body of Christ and it's a spiritual motivation. Often they are misunderstood – people believing they are only doing physical things. I am saying the gift itself is spiritual and the motivation to serve even though it is in ordinary ways is most necessary in the Body of Christ. The origin is in the spirit and the joy they get from it is in the Spirit of God. On this earth, it is a notable gift because giving service for free is rare. If we are consistent with our giving and serving, if we are consistent with our love, we will win them. We will eventually break down that wall between them and us so they will realize – we were genuine in our care. We were genuine in our love. Isn't that the message that Jesus would preach?

I do want to speak about what Jesus preached. He preached it not so much with words but with action. After the last supper – the feast of the Passover, supper being ended Jesus did something significant.

JESUS our Example

Usually, before supper began, the servants would wash the guests' hands and feet. The person of the lowest rank had to do this job. It was a dirty job. We no longer have that job in our society. They did not have sidewalks and concrete roads to walk on. Most of their travel was by foot. There was sand, dirt, mud camel dung etc. They literally had dirty feet.

What Jesus did literally is after supper, he took a towel and tied it around him. He poured water into a basin and knelt down at the disciples' feet. He took upon him the lowliest job possible. None of them understood at the moment what he was doing. He literally began to wash the disciples' feet. He did this on purpose choosing the lowest job to show true love through serving.

John 13: 12 So when He had washed their feet, and put on His garments, and sat down again, He said to them, "Do you know what I have done to you? 13 You call Me Teacher and Lord. You speak accurately, for so I am. 14 If I then, your Lord and Teacher, have washed your feet, you also ought to wash one another's feet. 15 For I have given you an example, that you should do as I have done to you. 16 Truly, truly I say to you, a servant is not greater than his master, nor is he who is sent greater than he who sent him. 17 If you know these things, blessed are you if you do them.

Literally he commanded us to do the same. They cannot understand. They have been following Him for three years knowing He is the Messiah. He is the chosen one. They esteemed Him so highly, how could He do such a lowly job? They believed He is the future King of Israel. That is who He was/that is who He is. Here he was doing a filthy job that only the lowest servant would do. We see the Apostle Peter hesitant as he says "You will never wash my feet. No way!" He believed Jesus was too good to do such a lowly thing.

Jesus responded that if Peter did not let Jesus wash his feet – He could have nothing from Him – that He had nothing to do with Him. In receiving the blessing of Jesus the servant, they were partakers of His cleansing of them – His love shown for them. Peter immediately responds – please serve me. Wash all of me. He wants to receive from Jesus – even though he cannot understand.

Jesus the Servant

This Jesus does to show He is the Servant King. He came to serve. He gave His life to die for us. He rose from the dead. He served us with His very life's blood. His life was servant ministry to us for three years as He taught and did miracles, He served us. He healed the sick; He cast our demons; He preached good news of the coming of the Kingdom of God. After His death, He ascended into heaven and poured His blood as an offering on the Mercy seat to cleanse us from all sin and unrighteousness.

The Sacrament of Foot Washing

Jesus is our example as the servant. Foot washing is an excellent way for us to give ourselves as servants. Some still practice it. I personally believe it – Jesus said blessed are you if you do these things. If there is any pride in a person before the foot washing, it isn't same after. Literally, if you give yourself in prayer and an attitude of prayer, washing your brother or sister's feet – it will disappear.

You may begin weeping. You may begin praising God as you pray blessings over the person whose feet you are washing. You want humility? This is an excellent way to get it. You cannot serve in the spirit and hold onto pride or arrogance of any kind. Are you getting too self- absorbed? Wash some feet. Start praying over those you are pouring water over their feet – start praying for them that God would bless them. God will use you and by your serving in this way you will experience a deep spiritual peace and joy as you obey the LORD.

You will not remain hard hearted and wash feet. Any hardness or bitterness any sin – you will repent immediately because you will realize "O God – I am serving You." The closest thing to this is the care a new mother has over her baby when it is first born. There is a deep humility knowing God has given you this soul to care for. Men also get it when they are feeding the baby, washing the baby, changing diapers etc. But it is your family, we expect this – in Foot washing – it doesn't have to be your family. It can be someone in church you hardly know. After you wash his or her feet – you will have a new love and respect for that person. [men with men in a separate place; women with women; married couples in a separate place].

To The Least of These

You serving someone who can never repay you – is you directly giving to Jesus Christ. God promises to bless those who consider the poor. I am not a Roman Catholic, but I want to give you an example of some one I highly regard and that is Mother Teresa of India. She had a good education and comfortable life in Europe. She gave herself to ministry as a nun. She chose to go to India and serve in the position.

I am going to describe it briefly. She literally would find children and babies that were abandoned on the streets that had diseases such as Aids. The babies were dying. If she and her team could help them to live they did, but a significant number of the children were dying. She would literally hold them, pray for them and love them before they died and while they were dying so that they knew someone cherished them. I believe the ministry of nuns she started is called daughters of Mercy. After she went, others started following.

Who would care for dying children that are abandoned on the street? She did and so did others with her. Who Cared? God cared. He touched their hearts so that order gave their lives to hold and care for dying children praying and thanking God for them, speaking words of love to them.

She is an example of extreme serving. Because she was a Roman Catholic, most people discount her any way. They believe that nuns and priests are not normal because they give their lives to care for others. The truth is she chose to serve.

A non-Roman Catholic Equivalent can be seen in Heidi and Roland Bakker in Mozambique. This highly educated American couple left a very comfortable life in California to go to war torn Mozambique to care for the poor orphans of that country. Literally, they feed thousands of people a day – mostly children who are war orphans. They were the first, now there are others who go and volunteer as missionaries with them in Iris ministry and there are branches of Iris ministry all over the world. Literally they feed, clothe, education, train, teach and spiritually minister to those orphans. Their lives are in peril because of the constant civil war and corruption in that nation.

Opportunities to Serve

There are missionary opportunities for people to literally build structures such as churches, schools, homes etc. The servants who go may teach or preach Christ in the evening but their purpose for going is to literally build buildings for the people. Physical serving of this kind is directly serving God by caring for others.

All Christians should have some element of serving in us because the Bible says we are to be hospitable, caring, giving. Jesus Christ lives in us so the there is some gift of serving in us. Not all Christians have it at the same level of strength or enjoy it the same. Some would rather preach or pray for people or evangelize, I understand there are different measures of the gift, but if we don't like serving at all, it is not Christian normal. Christians are the servants of God and we should be showing the love of God in some way by serving others. What we do on the earth we do with excellence, with diligence, serving to the best of our ability. Expect nothing in return from people. Expect that God will bless you as you serve.

Consecrate Yourself For Service

It is possible to consecrate yourself totally to service in the Body of Christ. It sounds controversial but it really means whole hearted commitment to God and in blessing the saints or the Church.
1 Corinthians 16: 15 You know the house of Stephanas, that it is the first fruits of Achaia, and that they have devoted themselves to the ministry of the saints.

Serving with Love

Their hearts were so overwhelmed with love that they desired to serve in the Body of Christ. One of the first things that happened to me when I became a Christian is I began to love Christians. I started sincerely caring about those around me in church. I started praying for the whole local church as though they were my family. If they were missing. I wanted to know if they were okay. In fact, I considered them my family. I started caring about the Church of Jesus Christ throughout the earth – those in other churches. Before I became a Christian, I didn't care about most Christians. There were one or two I could tolerate and not for very longer. I believed they were closed minded to other truths. Really, I was trying to make excuses for my sin.

Training Others to Serve

Some of the church teachers started training me in different aspects of ministry. They discipled me by pouring into me. They insisted that I join them in different outreaches such as nursing home and Bible class. They started stretching me to pray aloud in meetings, lead worship, lead people to Christ, pray for people who were water baptized.

In our church, we had to serve as part of the ministry training I took. I only believe it was positive for me because it gave me direct experience in areas I didn't really know much about such as teaching the toddlers. It made me realize how important those ministries were. I learned about the people; I learned that parents of young children have personal needs. If there is no child care in a church, and the children are crying, the parents leave the sanctuary and do not get spiritually built up. Those parents need spiritual teaching so they can manage all the aspects of their lives including raising their children. It is so important that Christian families get to hear the sermons and be able to worship freely.

Importance to Leaders

A person in ministry at a church needs to know about all the different areas in the church – all the different ministries. Even if you only go there for a short term, it will give you some idea of how valuable it is. You will get awareness of those ministries and their function in the church. Part of it also was the ministry itself was rewarding. I got to teach a group I had never taught before. I developed a true love for the children, seeing the kids growing, to see their parents and to pray for them and encourage them. That was personal ministry.

A second example was my serving in praying for those who were water baptized, to pray for the baptism of the Holy Spirit: praying for them before the water baptism, during and afterwards. It is a ministry. Those people are consecrating themselves to serve the LORD Jesus Christ for the rest of their lives. Praying for them is essential. They don't all have Christian families praying for them. They were taught and knew what water baptism is- not something to be taken lightly but a serious commitment to Christ. I not only knew the importance of the foundational teaching but had opportunity to serve helping others in their spiritual experience.

Helping Serve Helps the Pastors

Ministry training should show the fullness of the ministries within the

Church. We should have ministers that know the ministry that takes place beyond the pulpit. There are so many pastors that are pulled in so many directions; in small churches the pastor not only preaches but does visitation, evangelizes, sometimes does the cleaning and the mowing of the lawn etc. What if the body of that local church helped in each of those ministries so the pastor didn't have to do all of alone? I am talking about body ministry within and from the local church.

Some people actually have the wrong idea about pastors. They actually think the pastors are there to serve us – anything we want. The pastor is there to serve God. He or she is serving God by giving us the ministry of the Word. The appointing of the first deacons was to assist the pastors to help care for the widows and others.

Acts 6: 3 Brothers, look among yourselves for seven men who are known to be full of the Holy Spirit and of wisdom, whom we will appoint over this duty. 4 But we will give ourselves continually to prayer and to the ministry of the word."

We should have assistant pastors, helps for the pastors in all the aspects of ministry such as Evangelism, prayer, visitation, wise council, plus all the teaching and functions within the church. Pastors should be able to be home with their families also, not constantly be on duty.

The First Deacons

The disciples had much to share with people. They had over 3, 000 new converts that had to be taught about Jesus Christ the Messiah. They had personal stories to share about their being with Jesus for three years as He taught and preached and did miracles. They had to share the gospel message of Jesus Christ with as many people as they could, making disciples. Some of them had to write the gospels of the New Testament. It is because of these disciples and those who were taught by them that truths of Christ have been entrusted to us.

Notice the types of people they chose – spiritual, full of wisdom, given to the LORD. They were filled with the Holy Spirit and they were caring; they were known to be of good report. They had godly character to match. These were the ones chosen to minister in both the natural needs of people such as the widows and others. To be a servant, you must have wisdom to know if you should do it, if you shouldn't do it, if you are being taken advantage of etc.

You will notice that Stephan, who was stoned to death as the first Christian martyr of the was a deacon. He served; he preached; he lived his life sold out to God. The deacon was doing miracles. They should be spiritual plus they should be deacons. They serve God spiritually and concerning natural things as well.

Spiritual Servants

The servants in our church should be filled with the Holy Spirit and filled with faith operating in the supernatural. Give the best you can give knowing you are serving the LORD Jesus Christ.

God's model is always to have an elder teaching a younger. It's almost always one generation above – but not always.

Colossians 3: 23 And whatever you do, do it heartily, as for the Lord and not for men, 24 knowing that from the Lord you will receive the reward of the inheritance. For you serve the Lord Christ. 25 But he who does wrong will receive for the wrong which he has done, and there is no partiality.

Biblical Example

The optimum way to disciple is to have mentorship, personal caring discipleship by those slightly older or more spiritually mature than those they are teaching. As Moses trained Joshua, as Elijah trained Elisha, we should follow the model. For example, the older teenagers would be excellent to help with younger children if they are taught of the LORD and show spiritual maturity. I would even suggest paring an older teacher with a younger assistant to help. That way the person is directly trained and has guidance during their learning process in ministry.

Families Serving

Also, family ministry is so important. I literally mean, husbands and wives and children serving together in ministry in a local church. Servants will also train their families to serve. They will together help to do various tasks. This is an excellent model but not always possible because not always are complete families saved and committed to serving. It must be taught at home as a priority and reinforced at church.

Servants should train other young people. They should spiritually adopt first generation Christian teens and singles, and couples to serve alongside of them. Youth should be trained in serving. All age groups of the church should be taught to serve and given the opportunity.

1 Peter 4: 9 Show hospitality to one another without complaining.10 As everyone has received a gift, even so serve one another with it, as good stewards of the manifold grace of God. 11 If anyone speaks, let him speak as the oracles of God. If anyone serves, let him serve with the strength that God supplies, so that God in all things may be glorified through Jesus Christ, to whom be praise and dominion forever and ever. Amen.

5 MOTIVATION OF TEACHING

The motivation of teaching is a very strong desire clarify the truth: first to find the truth from God's Word; then to clarify it. This message is for born again spirit filled Christians baptized in the Holy Spirit. Those with the motivation gift of teaching will desire to seek what the Word of God says; they have a respect and reverence for God's Word. They will read it and study it comparing scripture with scripture. Often they will study the context of the passage and some will look up the origin of the meaning of words in Hebrew or Greek. Some may even study Hebrew and/or Greek so they can read the Bible in the original language. Usually they use an Amplified Bible because of the in depth explanation of each scripture.

They feel a strong desire to search for what God wants us to know from His Word. They can organize their research into chunks or lessons. They can organize their ideas into teachable units. Some do not pursue it further. They keep their own lesson plans for their own selves for further study etc. They do the research and perhaps share it with close friends or a spouse. Sometimes they do not publicly teach because they are shy.

The Characteristics of Teachers

Many teachers are very shy. By nature, teachers are very reserved people and find it hard to stand up in front of people. I do believe that with training and practice these people would be able to lead small or large Bible studies. Mentoring would make a difference in their lives. I actually believe a spiritual gift is never only for you. Some of these people I'm talking about have excellent notes – detailed and full of scripture. These people take notes in sermons at church. They document scriptures. These are as the Apostle Paul said were the Bereans who searched the scriptures themselves to see if it were true. They will not only take notes but go home and read them over and study them.

Some, teach Bible studies at their local church or in their homes. They are often context oriented. I have had several excellent Bible teachers who go into the passage and the exact reasons why it was given including history and sometimes archeology. Many pastors are highly motivated in the gift of teaching. They delight in passing on what they have learned from the LORD, sharing it with others. Pastors, by their very role have got to be able to plan their sermons. They must be able to communicate truths of God to the people. How much more would a pastor have to do it compared to a teacher? A pastor must prepare a Word that can feed the mature Christians, the teenagers, the new comers, those people from all areas and levels of Christian maturity. There must be something for the new Christians; there must be something for the seasoned saints.

Pastor/Teachers

The pastor/teacher can speak so the Word touches most of the people. It touches their hearts and encourages them. The pastor is like a master/teacher because they have to teach so many different types of people and also connect with them. Many pastors are teachers and that means the sheep would get a balanced diet of scripture from the old and new testaments with a Christ centered focus. Not all teachers because pastors. Some are at large churches and teach faithfully in their area of service. Some are assistant pastors; some lead small group Bible studies.

Often in our mega churches we have several pastors and some teach in various areas of expertise such as the doctrines of Christ, or spiritual gifts or particular books of the Bible. Often they will teach the truths that the particular congregation has light on.

Moses as Teacher

Moses was a tremendous teacher. We often don't think of Moses as a teacher because he was used as a Prophet of God. He directly heard God speak to him and give to him the commandments and the 613 commandments of Leviticus. Literally God dictated to them Word for word what to write. That is how we get the Torah or the books of Moses of the Old Testament. Moses was a friend of God and God shared His heart with Moses and His will for Israel. Moses had to teach those laws to the faithful priests in Israel who could teach it to others. Those laws and commandments had to be given to the people so they could understand it. God gave him specific instruction of how to build the Tabernacle in the wilderness. God gave Moses precise direction for the sacrifices and the manner of serving God.

The Israelites did not find a way to serve God. God instructed Moses as to how Israel should worship. Moses had to share those precise instructions with craftsmen who built the tabernacle. He had to explain it to Joshua and Caleb so they could continue the worship after Moses, so the people born in the wilderness could be raised to know the truths of God. Those in the Jewish faith or Messianic Christians would revere Moses as a teacher much more than we traditionally do.

Without Moses, we would not have the history of God's people spanning hundreds of years. Please understand, Moses was a different type of teacher. He directly received the Word of God from God Himself. Modern teachers rely on the Holy Spirit to guide them through the Bible which was written by direct inspiration of God. He was directly inspired by God to be a ministry teacher who would impart truths from God to the people of Israel in the past and for the present and for the future. God's Word was given to Moses so we could have it.

Deuteronomy 28 Now it will be, if you will diligently obey the voice of the Lord your God, being careful to do all His commandments which I am commanding you today, then the Lord your God will set you high above all the nations of the earth. 2 And all these blessings will come on you and overtake you if you listen to the voice of the Lord your God.

This scripture was given literally believing it would make a difference in their lives. They literally taught the Word of God to their children from their earliest years until they were grown and could teach others. Even today, many Jewish people have their children learning Hebrew so they can read the scriptures. Hopefully, we also are faithful to teach scripture to our children. Some denominations actually get their kids to memorize as much scripture as possible, believing that the more of God's Word we memorize, the more it will bless our lives.

The Same Truth of Emphasizing Scripture is Given.

Joshua 1: 8 This Book of the Law must not depart from your mouth. Meditate on it day and night so that you may act carefully according to all that is written in it. For then you will make your way successful, and you will be wise. 9 Have not I commanded you? Be strong and courageous. Do not be afraid or dismayed, for the Lord your God is with you wherever you go."

This passage instructs us that the Word of God should be so important to us that we think about it; we meditate on it; we think about the meaning of the words and the promises of God. It means we literally apply it to our lives and our hearts. It doesn't say it here but praying the Scripture is an awesome way to have the truths of Christ meaningful to us. It is an awesome way to meditate on the word of God – to pray it for ourselves and for others. These are examples of early teachers in Israel. Joshua was entrusted to keep the Word of God fresh before the people as a priority as he took them into the promised land.

Ezra The Scribe

Ezra is not often thought of a teacher but he brought restoration of the Word of God to the people. The prophet Ezra was a tremendous teacher who was used by God to turn Israel back to God. Ezra was in Babylon because of the captivity of Israel, but he goes with Nehemiah to instruct the people of Israel.

Ezra 7: 10 Because Ezra had prepared his heart to seek the Law of the Lord, he was doing so and teaching the statutes and judgments in Israel.

Ezra set himself apart to teach the word of God to others. Nehemiah 8 is one of my favourite passages because of the restoration of the Word of God to the people and their desire for the Word. The people of Israel are restored to their home land and here they are regathered; the walls have been rebuilt there; The people gathered themselves together as one man. That means they had a single purpose. They were in harmony; they wanted to know what was in the Word of God.

Ezra the scribe brought the book of Moses as he was commanded. There he reads the Word of God. He read the Word of God all morning until mid-day. He read the books of Moses nonstop. He wasn`t even preaching at first; he was just reading the word of God so the people could hear it. They had not heard it in over 70 years. Some of them had never heard it before. They didn`t have a written Bible as we have; they had scrolls that were hand written.

Israel had been in captivity; they did not have the freedom to worship God as they did here in Ezra.

Ezra 8: 5 Ezra opened the book in the sight of all the people (because he was above all the people), and, as he opened it, all the people stood up. 6 When Ezra blessed the Lord as the great God, all the people responded "Amen, Amen!" By lifting up their hands as they bowed their heads, they worshipped the Lord with their faces to the ground.

The people were excited to hear God`s Word, they lifted their hands in praise and kept shouting ``Àmen``. They worshipped and kept thanking God to hear His Word. The people were so thankful for Gods Word, they kept thanking God. They stood worshipping as the Word was read. They were thanking God for the Word of God restored to their lives. They were thanking God for the freedom to worship in Israel once again. They could pray; they could worship; they had been in captivity; now they were free.

The scripture says that Ezra caused them to know the meaning. The people stayed there all day. It was a teach-a-thon. Ezra read and taught the Word of God. Do you know what the response of the people was? They began to weep and cry knowing they had not kept the laws of God. As they heard the words they knew they were not living as God commanded. They were repentant and wept. It actually says that Ezra reproved them – he corrected them.

Ezra 8: "This day is holy to the Lord your God. Stop mourning and weeping." (This was because all the people wept when they heard the words of the Law.)

Ezra encouraged them to remember the Word of the Lord and to follow the Word from that day on. He encouraged them to go tell others of what they had learned. He commanded them to rejoice. This is Ezra`s teaching ministry to the restored of Israel. Ezra the scribe, faithfully read the Word of God to the people. There the Word of God was restored.

Jesus the Teacher

Perhaps the most awesome teacher is not in the Old Testament; it is Jesus Himself. In His three years of earthly ministry, from 30-33, He spent his life teaching, preaching, revealing the truth of God`s Word to the people. Miracles, signs and wonders were with Him – wherever He went.

Luke 11: 1 He was praying in a certain place, and when He ceased, one of His disciples said to Him, "Lord, teach us to pray, as John also taught his disciples."

The people acknowledge him and follow him as a teacher. They asked him to teach them to pray. He was doing miracles so they asked him to teach them to pray. They knew he knew how to touch God. They might not have known he was the Son of God but they knew he knew how to pray. He was called Rabbi – meaning teacher. He used parables to teach the people. Parables are stories comparing spiritual things to natural things – like analogies or allegories; stories that compare things and have depth to them that could give them understanding by their truths at a deeper level.

Jesus used every day examples from our lives such as planting, fishing, money etc. things ordinary people could relate to. Because He is the Living Word of God, He could explain the Words of Moses with practical application for the people. They loved him because the Word was made simple to apply to their lives. The disciples questioned him about his use of parables.

Matthew 13:10 The disciples came and said to Him, "Why do You speak to them in parables?"

11 He answered them, "It is given to you to know the mysteries of the kingdom of heaven, but to them it is not given. 12 For to him who has, will more be given, and he will have abundance. But from him who has not, even what he has will be taken away. 13 Therefore I speak to them in parables:

Jesus spoke to the people in every day language so they could understand. He spoke profound truths because He was one with God. Jesu went to synagogues, the Temple itself but also taught in the countryside and from a boat in the Sea because people followed Him so He taught them.

Jesus used the earth as His classroom. He used creation as examples because He is the Creator. He had a realm of teaching no other person could ever have. Some followed Jesus because of the miracles; some followed him out of curiosity; some followed Him for the teaching.

Luke 21: 37 Each day He was teaching in the temple, and each night He went out and stayed on the mountain called the Mount of Olives. 38 And all the people came early in the morning to hear Him in the temple.

Jesus' Illustrated Sermons

Jesus' illustrated sermons were the most awesome sermons the earth has ever known. This is one of Jesus` illustrated sermon. He is teaching in Matthew 12. He is teaching in the synagogue. People are not suppose to do any work on the Sabbath day because it was a Holy day. Jesus the Living Word is standing in the synagogue. Jesus the Living Word is showing us the meaning of the Word. He sees a man with a withered hand and is moved by mercy and compassion. The people watched him – especially the Pharisees to see if he would break the law and heal on the Sabbath. They did not understand the heart of the law – given by God`s mercy to us to be light for our lives.

Matthew 12: 9 When He had departed from there, He went into their synagogue. 10 And there was a man whose hand had withered. They asked Him, "Is it lawful to heal on the Sabbath?" that they might accuse Him.

11 He said to them, "What man is there among you who has one sheep, and if it falls into a pit on the Sabbath, will not lay hold of it and lift it out? 12 Then how much better is a man than a sheep? Therefore, it is lawful to do good on the Sabbath." 13 Then He said to the man, "Stretch out your hand."

Jesus emphasizes the importance of mercy and says to the man with the withered hand, `Stretch forth your hand``. The Pharisees were so outraged that he healed on the Sabbath because they were blinded by legalism. They did not rejoice with the man being healed. Jesus illustrated sermon shows the mercy of God and the law of God. He is the Living Word. He is teaching the Word in the synagogue showing that God`s mercy for one who needed healing was stronger than the law itself. Jesus said He is the Lord of the Sabbath.

The other example I`d like to give you is in Mark 2. Jesus was teaching in a home and so many people were gathered there was no room for any people. Some friends brought their friend, carried on a stretcher because he was paralyzed. They actually believed if they could get their friend to Jesus, he could be healed. They actually had faith. They had no way to get there. There was no way to get through to Jesus. They literally dug a hole in the roof and lowered their friend down at the feet of Jesus. Jesus saw the men's`` faith. He said to the paralytic: Your sins be forgiven you. `He is showing Himself as Messiah here. He forgave the man his sins. Of course this outraged the people who did not know He is Messiah. They accused him of blasphemy. Jesus knows their thoughts and actually speaks to them asking what is easier to forgive sins or heal. Well the truth was those men could do neither. Only Jesus could do both.

Mark 2: When they could not come near Him due to the crowding, they uncovered the roof where He was. When they had broken it open, they let down the bed on which the paralytic lay. 5 When Jesus saw their faith, He said to the paralytic, "Son, your sins are forgiven you."

6 But some of the scribes were sitting there, reasoning in their hearts, 7 "Why does this Man speak such blasphemies? Who can forgive sins but God alone?" 8 Immediately, when Jesus perceived in His spirit that they so reasoned within themselves, He said to them, "Why do you contemplate these things in your hearts? 9 Which is easier to say to the paralytic: 'Your sins are forgiven you,' or to say, 'Rise, take up your bed and walk'? 10 But that you may know that the Son of Man has authority on earth to forgive sins," He said to the paralytic, 11 "I say to you, rise, and take up your bed, and go your way to your house." 12 Immediately he rose, picked up the

bed, and went out in front of them all, so that they were all amazed and glorified God, saying, "We never saw anything like this!"

Jesus said this miracle was so that the people would know he had the power to forgive sins also. As soon as Jesus spoke healing to the man, he was made well. He got up and everyone was amazed at the miracle of God. Jesus` illustrated sermons were miraculous. They were not only temporary. They were the words of God spoken through Moses – being fulfilled by Jesus in the present moment. The RHEMA Word of God standing there revealing Himself as creator, healer, Messiah.

In John 3 we have a faithful, truthful searching Pharisee; it is Nicodemus who comes to Jesus and calls him Rabbi. He acknowledges him as a teacher and respects him saying no one could do these mighty miracles unless God was with Him. He is well respected. This shows Nicodemus` heart wanted to know the truth. Jesus spoke to him the meaning of the scriptures.

In Luke 10, a legalistic man came asking how he could gain eternal life. Luke 10: 26 He said to him, "What is written in the law? How do you read?"

27 He answered, " 'You shall love the Lord your God with all your heart, and with all your soul, and with all your strength, and with all your mind'[a] and 'your neighbor as yourself.'[b]"

Jesus told him he had answered correctly. Jesus interpreted Moses for us saying yes this was the heart and core of the law. The man had a good answer. His answer showed that he had memorized the important part of the law. But the man also revealed his desire to justify himself in his words.

Matthew 16: 27 For the Son of Man shall come with His angels in the glory of His Father, and then He will repay every man according to his works.

Jesus was speaking to his disciples so that they would know who he is. Some said one thing. Some said another. Only Peter has the revelation of Jesus a Messiah at that moment.

Matthew 27: 16 Simon Peter replied, "You are the Christ, the Son of the living God."

Afterwards Jesus shares with his disciples he must go to Jerusalem and die and be raised from the dead. Peter does not understand and tries to tell him he should not do this. He is rebuked by Jesus. Peter doesn`t understand that what Jesus is saying is not what could be but it is what must be – Jesus is prophesying about Himself in fulfillment of Messianic Prophecy (Is 53) Even though he is in the confines of a human body, Jesus is speaking beyond time or space. He is speaking destiny proclamations fulfilling the demands of the law of a sacrifice for sin.

Matthew 27: 22 Then Peter took Him and began rebuking Him, saying, "Far be it from You, Lord! This shall not happen to You."

23 But He turned and said to Peter, "Get behind Me, Satan! You are an offense to Me, for you are not mindful of the things that are of God, but those that are of men."

Jesus is a man, who never sinned, who lived a Holy life, who came to earth to die in our place as our Messiah or Saviour. The disciples do not understand as he is speaking but they remembered it afterwards. They did not have the God breathed understanding that God was connecting with them about They did not have the God breathed understanding that God was connecting with them about eternal truths and fulfillment of prophesy. It was beyond all human understanding and knowledge. Only by revelation did it come to them later. Jesus, the Living Word, emphasizing his prophetic life and purpose to those closest to him was imparting into them truths that would be so deep – it would cause them, after his resurrection, to write the New Testament and to go to the nations preaching this good news.

The disciples were perhaps hoping for a triumphal entry into Jerusalem that would proclaim Jesus as Messiah and he would set up his earthly kingdom. Jesus taught them he was returning here in

Luke 21: 27 Then they will see the Son of Man coming in a cloud with power and great glory. 28 When these things begin to happen, look up and lift up your heads, for your redemption is drawing near."

He explains signs of the times of his return. The disciples want to understand what he is saying. They want to know the sign of the end of the age. Jesus is instructing them that he will return. In his ascension in the book of Acts, the angels declare to those , over 500 witnesses, who watch him visibly ascend up into heaven. The angels declare the return of Christ as well.

Acts 1: 11 They said, "Men of Galilee, why stand looking toward heaven? This same Jesus, who was taken up from you to heaven, will come in like manner as you saw Him go into heaven."

The RHEMA Word

Christ the teacher lives in us. The most awesome types of preaching is the preaching of the God breathed inspired Word. God reveals the meaning of the scriptures to you. Those with the motivation of teaching get spiritual gems or spiritual nuggets as God quickens the meaning of the scriptures to them – usually comparing scripture with scripture.

Teachers, search the Word of God and see the corresponding passages and other scriptures related. Oh yes. Compare the Greek with the different English versions. Compare the Hebrew with the different English translations but don`t forget the author. The Holy Spirit is the author of the scripture. He inspired holy men of God to write it. The Holy Spirit is the teacher; He can teach us by quickening the truth of it to us and how it applies to our lives. Don`t forget to invite the Holy Spirit into your Bible study so that you will be able to impart the truths of it to others. Oh the RHEMA Word of God – is God Himself bringing revelation of the Scriptures to us in the present moment directly applying it to our lives.

As Ezra was a teacher, as the Apostle Paul was a teacher, you can be that inspired teacher to help others understand the truths of the Word of God. Pray for inspiration of the scriptures. Don`t simply teach what your doctrine teaches in your denomination. Find it out for yourself. Ask the Holy Spirit to quicken the meaning to you.

The Word of God is quick, powerful, sharper than any two edged sword, piercing between joints and marrow, a discerner of the thoughts and intents of the heart. Hebrews 4: 12-13

The Word of God is so awesome in its manifold beauty that you can read a scripture one day and you can read the same scripture the next day and God can breathe on it and new meaning, fresh revelation of meaning can come to you. Like God provided for Israel in the wilderness, fresh bread – fresh manna each day for forty years, God can give you fresh revelation of his Word each day, so that it can give you life for that day and more than enough so that you could share it with others. Don't forget to ask the Author of the Scriptures for understanding.

Spirit Anointed Teachers

Jesus reproves some who studied the scriptures searching for the truth, who ignored the author of the scriptures. We must be spirit filled teachers of the Word of God. We must be Spirit led teachers; we must ask the LORD for anointing so that we can teach the Word of God.

The Apostle Paul, I can`t say if he is the best, but He is most certainly an excellent example of a New Testament teacher. He is certainly an awesome example. As God did with Moses, so he did with the Apostle Paul, inspiring him to write most of the New Testament. Those who wrote the scriptures, were inspired by God Himself so that the Word of God would be written for us, thousands of years later. But also so that those who received the word of God could be inspired to share the Word of God with the men and women and children around them imparting to them the truths of God so they would never be forgotten.

A teacher will care about facts, accuracy, so the truths can be imparted. One famous scripture is as follows:

Study to show yourself approved, rightly dividing the word of truth. 2 Timothy 2: 15

Teach prayerfully, asking from God, listening to God, studying, listening to other respected teachers of the faith. Press into them to learn from them. Here is Paul instructing Timothy. Some of my favourite scripture is in Timothy. Paul led him to Christ and taught him scripture and trained him to lead a church.

2 Tim 2: 2 Share the things that you have heard from me in the presence of many witnesses with faithful men who will be able to teach others also.

Again the same thing that was in the Old Testament is here. Teach and teach others who will teach others. Keep teaching the truths to the children to be passed on to the future generations.

2 Tim 2: 24 The servant of the Lord must not quarrel, but must be gentle toward all people, able to teach, patient, 25 in gentleness instructing those in opposition.

The teacher is to impart truth. We should not be arguing about meaning. Teachers should be with people who desire to know the truth. In other places he warns them – to have nothing to do with people who are contentious. They are trying to bring strife. (Romans 16: 17)

Ministers should be able to teach their congregations. Ministers should remain humble. As we ordain ministers, these teaching impartation scriptures are usually read over them as they are prayed for.

2 Timothy 3: 16 All Scripture is inspired by God and is profitable for teaching, for reproof, for correction, and for instruction in righteousness, 17 that the man of God may be complete, thoroughly equipped for every good work.

It is so clear here that we are to take the scriptures and apply them to all areas of our lives. It is for how we are to live, how we are to worship, how we are to interact with others. It is the book- the manual for life for people on the earth – a user guide. Teachers are able to examine it and dig precious truths and present them to us so we can understand them.

There are many people who would like to compartmentalize our lives, saying this much of activity, this much social, this much God… as though you could fit God into a box.

Motivated to Share Truth

Teachers are motivated to share with others the truth of the Word of God. Let God be the one to show you what to do in life and how to live your life. Let respected elders in the faith give you wise counsel from the Word of God. Let the Word of God be the plumb line setting the standard for your life – the foundation for your life, that you might be a Temple of the Holy Spirit living Holy for Him. Not every person with the motivation of teaching is going to be in ministry full time; some will teach a Bible class; some will teach children; some will teach adults; some will teach small groups. There are all levels of motivation for teaching in ministry.

I heard Lester Sumrall, an anointed teacher of the Word as well as Evangelist and prophet of God; this man of God in his 70`s and 80`s was wearing out the young people who he was training up because he was so compelled to pass on the Word of God from country to country, from meeting to meeting. He was compelled to preach, teach and impart to as many as possible the things that God had taught him. He had such a drive within him that nothing could hold him back. Others his age were rocking and relaxing; but this man of God was anointed and knew the things God had taught him had to be imparted to others.

We only have one life. Find out what God wants you to do. If it is the motivation of teaching, obey. Is it a Sunday school class? Don`t take it lightly. It is an honourable thing. Do it with all your heart. Give your best as unto God. I thank God for the vacation Bible school teacher that taught about Jesus dying for our sins so we could be saved. I was only five years old but I knew it was important. I had no prior knowledge and received no further teaching for almost 16 years, but that lady led me to the LORD and God remembered my prayer that day. That teacher had a faithful heart to impart truths to 5-year-old children something eternal. She took her ministry most seriously and prayerfully. She was Holy Spirit lead to lead us in prayer to the LORD. She didn't get us doing anything weird. She made a way to teach those truths to us and communicate at our level so we could understand.

A Family of Teachers and Preachers

Don`t take any ministry lightly. What you do, do it with excellence. And honour. Seek the LORD and ask Him if He wants you to teach in your home. Tremendous teachers of this century, The Copeland family, who carry the truths of God from those before them, who travel the world, preaching and teaching the Word of God with faith. The whole family is consecrated, set apart to teach and preach the Word of God. It could be your family. Teach your children to minister at an early age and train them up in ministry. The book of Leviticus is full of teaching priests. Whole families were set apart for the glory of God. As things can be in your DNA, so can the anointing be upon a family, to teach God`s Word.

Seek the LORD for yourself. What would God have you to do? A prophet of God might confirm the Word of God to you but only God can impart to you directly what you and your family should do regarding ministry. Press into God to ask Him what He would have you to do. Present yourself to God for His service. Prayer for opportunity.

The Apostle Paul had a prayer request – he prayed for doors of utterance – opportunities to preach Christ. (Colossians 4: 3)

Pray for yourself for doors of utterance, that you will be able to use your gifts for God.

In Timothy, we see Paul`s protégé who passed the truths on to others. It was passed on for 2, 000 years to us – faithfully by Christians, some of them martyred for their faith. Some of them hiding the scriptures so they could be preserved for us. Some of them didn`t have all the scrolls of the

Bible, but what they did have, they preached and taught faithfully. O Our Bible was brought together by the anointing of the LORD. If you have a motivation for teaching the Word of God – what a high calling to be entrusted to teach the truths of the Word of God to people.

6 EXHORTATION

Exhortation comes from the same root Greek word Paraclete which is the word for the Holy Spirit which means to come along side and assist, to encourage, to bring faith, to restore, to encourage and sometimes teach as well. This particular gift has some of the same qualities as the Holy Spirit Himself.

Usually the person who has this gift is very outgoing and people oriented. They enjoy speaking with people, encouraging others etc. I would like to examine the example that I know of in scripture. It is the example of Moses' wife's father who notices Moses trying to lead all by himself – over 2 million people.

They did not have the technology we have so it was not as organized as it could have been. There were huge line ups of people waiting to speak with him. Some of the matters were insignificant. Others were important. Moses did not have the revelation of what to do so he tried to do all the work of the ministry alone. Jethro observed this and God gave him a word of wisdom about the situation to help Moses solve the situation. God use him to speak it to Moses and Moses saw the advice was good and listened to Jethro.

Exodus 18: "What you are doing is not good. 18 You will surely wear yourself out, both you, and these people who are with you, for this thing is too heavy for you. You are not able to do it by yourself. 19 Now listen to me, I will advise you, and may God be with you: You be a representative for the people to God so that you may bring their disputes to God. 20 And you shall teach them the statutes and laws and shall show them the way in which they must walk and the work that they must do. 21 Moreover, you shall choose out of all the people capable men who fear God, men of truth, hating dishonest gain, and place these men over them, to be rulers of thousands, rulers of hundreds, rulers of fifties, and rulers of tens. 22 Let them judge the people at all times, and let it be that every difficult matter they shall bring to you, but every small matter they shall judge, so that it will be easier for you, and they will bear the burden with you. 23 If you shall do this thing and God commands you so, then you will be able to endure, and all these people also will go to their place in peace."

Moses listened to Jethro and shared the ministry with other leaders of thousands, hundreds etc. This solved the issue of long line ups as well as Moses having to deal with so many people.

Exhorters – truly flowing in the gift are inspired with ideas from God – are inspirational encouragement, solutions and advice. God uses them to speak wisdom and insight into people's lives to help others to solve issues in their lives.

Pastors of large churches have to do the same thing. There are mega churches of 20, 000 or 30, 000 people. Churches of 1, 000 members are not so rare. There is no possible way for the pastors, even if there is a team of twenty pastors, to minister to all the needs of the people. They must have helpers to share the ministry tasks and responsibilities. They have elders and deacons and cell group leaders who care for the people. It is a way of being accountable and handling matters in a large congregation.

Exhortation to Fear Not

This situation with Moses is special. It was a huge burden to Moses but Moses didn't think of answer. God didn't directly speak to Moses an answer. Please notice that God didn't reveal it to Moses. Some things God expects us to solve etc. In this case though, God used Jethro to give godly advice.

Exodus 14: 13 But Moses said to the people, "Fear not! Stand firm! And see the salvation of the Lord, which He will show you today. For the Egyptians whom you have seen today, you shall never see again. 14 The Lord shall fight for you, while you hold your peace."

Moses actually spoke peace as He lead the people. They were pursued by Pharaoh until they reached the Red Sea. It was here that the people were fearful and accused Moses and God of leading them to death, Moses was inspired by God to speak these words of comfort and peace to the people. Notice he said "Fear not". Moses has a godly response. He does not speak anger or any soulish thing. He speaks an inspired word from God. Fear was the root of the people's murmuring and accusations. They were fearful and it could have lea to their death. Moses inspired faith by speaking over the people that God Himself would fight for them. Fear Not shows insight and a word of wisdom.

Fear in a crowd of two million could most certainly lead to panic and death. You may have heard of certain stadiums filled with people where something happens and the people stampede and trample others. Fear spreads and causes people to react strangely. Moses not only speaks against fear but inspires faith. After Moses words, Moses raises his shepherd's rod and the Red Sea parts.

Encouragers may be people you know, people in your life but they can also be people God inspires that you have never met before. There have been so many phenomenal encouragers in moments where fear could have spread. These people are our heroes. They react in extreme circumstances with faith and they calm and comfort the people around them.

Todd Beamer

In 2001, on September 11, Todd Beamer was such a person. He actually gave his life to defend his country and stop terrorists plans to crash a jet into the White House. Literally, he and his friends encouraged each other to overtake armed terrorists and attempt to land the plane. As they did, he was noted for praying, reciting the LORD's prayer and Psalm 23 and encouraging the passengers abound that plane. He was given supernatural strength in an extreme situation.

This is an extreme example of an encourager. Please know most people don't face these situations, but God will use an encourager in such situations to bring peace and comfort to the people there. In a moment of decision, he made the decision to be filled with faith and try to comfort the people as they overthrew armed terrorists. They crashed the plane rather than let it hit in Washington. It meant their death but stopped an attack on the country's capital.

There have been people like this in battle, in war, in horrendous situations that God uses to shine valour and honour in and through. He uses people to speak peace and bring comfort to those around them. God will inspire faith, courage, even if it means facing death. There are books on these topics about heroes who save lives, give encouragement and comfort to people in extreme circumstances. Recently in the media there have been reports of teachers who stop a crazed shooter in their schools by overtaking them to protect the students and everyone else. We honour such people in North America with awards of Valour and Honour.

Usual Gift of Encouragement

Most encouragers come along side people as though they know they should minister to those people. For instance, you could be clearing a table at church after a banquet and an encourager will begin to speak to you. You will most certainly know if it occurs because he or she will begin directly to zone in on you and whatever issue is bothering you. Usually the root is fear. It could be a negative situation in your life or something you are praying about and need wisdom about.

The Encourager usually flows in the gifts of word of wisdom and word of knowledge. They may also operate in the gift of prophetic encouragement. They will speak to you not at a natural level but directly to your spirit. As they share with you, you will feel as though the Holy Spirit is lifting you out of your problem and causing you to see from a different point of view. The words are like a healing balm. They comfort you in ways that are hard to explain in natural terms. God inspires them to give you wise counsel. God uses them to give you a solution. Often there are stages or steps to the solution.

David

Jonathan comforted David in such a way. David had been an armour bearer for king Saul. He carried the armour and put the armour on the king. Also, he played the harp and sang songs to comfort the king. After Saul had disobeyed God, God's spirit left him and an evil spirit tormented him. He was comforted by David's singing and playing of the harp.

The anointing on David brought peace to Saul. The Spirit of the LORD was on David. He was anointed. Everything he did, he did with an excellent spirit and to the glory of God. He served the king faithfully and became best friends with Saul's son Jonathan. The angels of the LORD would have been surrounding David. They would have brought peace to the atmosphere as David was with Saul.

The anointed music of king David was a blessing to the king but also David was flowing with the Spirit of God. His heart was pure and right. He thought of what was best for the king and for Israel. David was a hero. He fought in Saul's army and won victories for Israel. Instead of viewing David as a loyal, faithful servant, Saul became possessed with jealousy. He hated David because David was good. He hated David because the anointing of the LORD was on David.

The evil spirit that possessed Saul got hold of Saul in a strange way. While they were at supper, Saul hurled a javelin to try to kill David. David ran for his life. He did not understand it. He did not deserve it. He was only loyal, kind, caring and he loved Saul faithfully. David was pure. He did not provoke it in any way. David knew his life was at risk, even though he didn't understand.

David ran into the wilderness and this is where Jonathan comes to comfort him. At first Jonathan didn't believe it could be true. He could not believe his father would kill David. It was such a demonic thing that it made no natural sense. The captain of the army, a member of the royal family (he married Saul's daughter), a friend and a confident of their family – why would Saul try to kill him? Jonathon did not believe it and decided to see if it was true for himself.

God uses Friends as Encouragers

What is usual about this gift of encouragement is that Jonathan is a close friend of David. He brings words of encouragement to strengthen David's heart. Our best ways of encouraging each other as Christian friends is to speak God's word to each other, do things for each other etc. It is here where David is hiding in the woods for his life that Jonathan comes and speaks words to encourage him. Please notice again, the words "fear not". As that is always the most important thing to get rid of first. Also, he speaks safety and peace over him and even confirms David's promises from God to him (prophetic words from the prophet Samuel to David of his becoming the king) and comes into agreement with him.

Jonathan

1 Samuel 23: 15 Now David saw that Saul had come out to seek his life. And David was in the Wilderness of Ziph in Horesh. 16 Jonathan, the son of Saul, arose and went to David at Horesh. And he strengthened his hand in God. 17 He said to him, "Do not fear, for the hand of Saul my father will not find you. You will be king over Israel, and I will be next to you. Saul my father knows this." 18 The two of them made a covenant before the Lord. And David stayed in Horesh, but Jonathan went to his house.

If God gives you an opportunity to be an encourager to someone, remind the person of the promises of God to him or her. You will sense that the Holy Spirit is using you. Speak scripture to the person. Prayerfully minister kind words.

Jehoshophat

This next example is a prophetic encourager to King Jehosophat in a terrible situation where the people were to be attacked by the enemy and fear could have caused them to panic. Jehoshaphat literally spreads out the threatening letter from the enemy before the LORD and prays asking for a miracle. God send Jehoshaphat to encourage him. Notice again – he says "fear not". That is the first priority. In fear, people do not act properly. Faith in God's Word is the weapon used to defeat the enemy. After the fear not – a prophetic word of victory is given.

2 Chronicles 20: 14 And in the midst of the assembly the Spirit of the Lord came on Jahaziel the son of Zechariah, the son of Benaiah, the son of Jeiel, the son of Mattaniah, a Levite from the line of Asaph.

15 And he said, "Pay attention all Judah, and those dwelling in Jerusalem, and King Jehoshaphat: Thus says the Lord to you, 'Do not fear, nor be dismayed because of this great army, for the battle is not yours, but God's. 16 Tomorrow, go down against them. They will travel up by the Ascent of Ziz. You will find them at the back of the valley, before the Wilderness of Jeruel. 17 It will not be necessary for you to fight in this conflict. Take your positions, stand, and observe the deliverance of the Lord for you, O Judah and Jerusalem.' Do not fear or be filled with terror. Tomorrow, go out before them, and the Lord will be with you."

Barnabus and Saul

In the book of Acts there is a disciple called Barnabus; his very name means son of consolation or comforter and encourager. The Apostle Paul had received prophesy from God concerning him witnessing to the Gentiles (non- Israelites who were mostly pagans) and winning them to Christ.

The Apostle Peter has a divine revelation and realizes that God is pouring out the Spirit not only on the Jews but also the Gentiles. Peter is used to minister to Cornelius a Roman Centurion and his family. They received Christ and the Baptism of the Holy Spirit. The first response from the early church was to question why Gentiles should be let into the church because they were considered unclean. As Peter explains God's moving among the Gentiles, Barnabus sets sail for Tarsus to find the apostle Paul. He remembered that Paul had the prophetic word over him.

There is no other record of disciples contacting Paul until this spot in Acts 15.

Acts 15: 22 Then it pleased the Apostles and the elders, with the whole church, to send chosen men from among them to Antioch with Paul and

Barnabas, namely, Judas called Barnabas, and Silas, leading men among the brothers.

Paul and Barnabus strengthened each other in ministry each other and went to Antioch to preach to the Gentiles the good news of salvation through Jesus Christ. They stayed there for quite some about a year time winning souls and discipling them. It was at Antioch that we get our name Christian. Before that the term Christian isn't used. The Antioch church is famous for sending missionaries to other lands and for sending finances to help the Jews in Jerusalem.

Often the encourager is a friend. In this instance Paul and Barnabus encouraged each other and shared the ministry of Christ enduring hardships such as beatings, stonings, imprisonment, shipwreck etc.

Proverbs 27: 17 Iron sharpens iron,
  so a man sharpens the countenance of his friend.

True Christian Friends

A true Christian friend will give us godly counsel. He or she will pray for us. We Christians should be encouraging each other, praying for each other in person – not just praying for someone but praying with the people. True spiritual Christian friends will not agree with any negatively. In fact, the Christian friend will correct you and point to God's Word as hope and to inspire faith. If there is a problem, the Christian friend points to the solution and sincerely prays for an answer. Literally one should pray, how can I be a good Christian friend? How can I encourage my friend in the LORD? It is most common God will use your spouse or a Christian relative or a Christian friend to speak encouragement to you.

Unique Opportunities

There are instances that are different. There are sometimes assignments that God will give you by placing certain people in your life – even briefly. On one occasion I was with a friend and he went into a card shop – I saw a Pet shop and loving animals, decided I would go in. as I walked around, God zoomed me in on an older lady perhaps in her 60's and her daughter who were shopping for a pet dog.

I strongly felt God prompting me to go speak to her, Please know I did not know her and had no idea of what to say. I was certain God was impressing on me that woman needed a word of encouragement. I wandered around hoping God would speak something to me directly. Nothing specific came. Finally, after so many minutes, they were in line to purchase the dog etc. I stood behind them with some insignificant purchase.

I obeyed God by making kind and friendly comments to them. Suddenly in the midst of the friendly chatter I knew God was speaking to me directly I said to the woman, " God wants you to know He cares for you very much and He hears your prayers." Something very similar... She had tears in her eyes. Her daughter explained that her father had recently died leaving her mother alone and that they had praying very much for strength. I wish I could say I did more. I didn't.

What I did do is obey the LORD. I spoke the .words he gave me and I know they touched the woman and her daughter deeply. I also know I had no natural knowledge of the situation. I thanked God completely for the opportunity to encourage and speak hope to someone.

Be Equally Yoked

Pastors almost always have a gift of encouragement. Usually they share Christ and speak peace and comfort to the congregation as a whole. Those close around us are usually used in personal situations. We should surround ourselves with people of faith. Our closest friends should be Christians. We have no business being yoked to unbelievers in close relationships. It is not only for marriage. It applies to all close relationships.

An ungodly friend is not going to give you godly advice. People who are living in the Eon, the age, with the spirit of the age – living in the soulish realm are never going to give you godly spiritual advice. Who you choose to be around you determines the type of life input you will have. There are foolish people who live by the world's standards. Do not let them in your close circle of friends.

Believe me, an ungodly person will give you worldly advice. Your husband or wife left you? Go get drunk; Go have sex, You can find somebody else. This is the type of advice those people would give you because that is the standard the world lives by.

Even among Christians we should be choosey on who we let in our lives. There are carnal Christians who will be negative or dump on you. What I mean is they talk about negative things' they say nasty, stupid stuff, anything that comes to them. They don't care about improving their lives and don't listen to godly advice. These people are best outside of our lives.

Encouragers Get Dumped On

I am going to tell you that encouragers are sometimes dumped on – taken advantage of. Even if the encourager gives prayerful, godly wisdom, some people do not want to change and will not listen to godly advice. These are people that should have no place in your life. Literally dumping – or ranting or complaining and negativity could discourage almost anyone, but someone with the gift of encouragement who literally prays for godly wisdom to give and is ignored – it is rejecting the gift of God offered through them and they should cut off those relationships.

In 2nd Peter the term like precious faith is used in the King James version – these are people who believe the same, who live the same, who are spiritually living for Jesus.

In 2 Peter 1: 1 …To those who have received a faith as precious as ours through the righteousness of our God and Savior Jesus Christ.

If a Christian has a tragedy or situation that is overwhelming, a Christian friend should be speaking words of life and hope and healing and faith to that friend. We should tolerate no negativity, no self pity, no fear etc in ourselves or in our friends.

The best possibility is that we should comfort ourselves in the LORD, praying, praising worshipping, seeking God for an answer etc.

Ziglag

David found himself in a terrible situation. The grief of the situation was horrible. The city he was living in had been destroyed. The women and children were taken as captives. The men of the city who were with David talked of stoning him because they blamed him for the enemy's attack on their home. They wept until they could weep no more.

1 Samuel 30: But David encouraged himself in the Lord his God.

This is a mighty statement. In spite of all the negative news, David remembered His God is really God. After he stirs up his own faith, he enquires of the LORD believing God could give him a solution.

1 Samuel 30: 7 And David said to Abiathar the priest, the son of Ahimelek, "Please bring the ephod to me." So Abiathar brought the ephod to David. 8 David inquired at the Lord, saying, "Should I pursue after this raiding party? Will I overtake them?"

And He answered him, "Pursue them, for you will surely overtake them and will surely recover all."

Truly this causes joy and faith to come to David. One Word from God can totally transform any situation. God is a God of resurrection life, of hope, of faith, of joy.

Encourage Yourself

That is what we as Christians must do. Our spirit man should be strongest. If necessary, we should get hold of our soul (our mind, will and emotions) and body and bring it into alignment with God's Word. It means living in the spirit, living in the presence of God.

In the World but not of the World

A Christian that is fearful is not right. A Christian who is negative is not right. A Christian who is complaining is not right. All these things are garbage, polluted water. Fear, doubt, unbelief, hatred, jealousy, envy, bitterness... We should have zero tolerance concerning all these things. If we pick up any trace of any of these in our friend, we should pray immediately because that person is under attack. We should pray for God to give us words to say to speak life to our friends. Those things are symptoms that their spirit is under attack.

A Christian doesn't live in the realm of the everyday person. The climate of the world, this age is given to fear and panic and media driven fear mongers. They have systems in our world that are built on fear. The economy feeds off your fear, covetousness, jealousy, envy etc. . The news, the reports etc. can be negatively and are completely from the point of view of man living in a fallen world – negative. These things cannot be a part of our lives. We should have zero tolerance for any of these things in us or in those close to us.

In order to be free of these things, we can't listen to music that promotes fear or sin. We can't put before our eyes things that are ungodly. We can't go places God wouldn't approve of us going to, we cannot break the laws of od or the laws of our land and keep free of this garbage. Those things are the from the devil. That's not our source. We were not meant to live with any of it.

None of the people on earth are meant for any of those things but the non-Christians do not have the freedom to day no. They are in bondage and don't know any other way. They don't know they are in bondage to those things. They don't know that it is a chain that binds them and makes them fearful and fleshly and stops them from receiving God's best. The godly way seems foolish to them.

Joyce Meyer's Example

One of the best examples of this is given by Joyce Meyer. I heard it and believe it is an excellent example of how much of sin we should tolerate. I quote her to give her credit but this is my memory in paraphrase. If you have not heard her, I highly recommend you listen to or watch her. She herself had a horrendous life and God delivered her out of it, gave her an awesome testimony healed her, blessed her, uses her to encourage others. Testimonies are life truths of miracles God has done for you. She teaches the word of God knowing what it is like to be totally healed by God. God has given her favour with many people to share Christ.

She doesn't allow one grain of fear, doubt, unbelief , strife etc., in her life. She spoke on one occasion of saying to people who say – it isn't that bad. There is only a little bit of it (fear, doubt, unbelief, ungodliness) as a way for allowing a little darkness into their lives. A little bit – that's not so bad, right? What if we allow a tiny bit? After all you don't want to be too heavenly minded… There are carnal Christians who will say, you don't have to be all Christian, you can be partly saved and partly in the world…you can ride the border…

She says I'm going to bake some chocolate chip cookies. Do you want some? Everybody says yes.

Then she says " Is it ok if I put a little poop in there? I won't put much – only a little poop. You won't even taste it. You will know it's there, but is a little poop ok? You could still enjoy the cookie. It will still be good."

That is utterly disgusting to all of us but it is such an awesome example of how much sin, fear, envy, strife etc. we should tolerate. We should allow none. In our friends we should allow none. I'm talking about spirit filled born again believers baptized in the Holy Spirit. We should live by a different standard.

Inspirational is word that comes to me when I think of the encouragers God has put in my life. They are people who cause you to dream big, to do excellently and to achieve your goals. I am talking about doing that which is right, that which is pure, that which is godly, that which is Holy.

Paul and Barnabus

Paul and Barnabus are travelling together. Their mission base was Antioch. Wherever the Spirit of God is moving, there are going to be prophets there. The Antioch Church had within it prophets, apostles, pastors, teachers, evangelists – the five-fold ministry was evident there. They would go from church to church preaching, teaching, building up, establishing. It was dynamic; it was vibrant. The different gifts would work together to plant churches and establish believers.

During a period of fasting and prayer, there was a moving of the Holy Spirit. They were separating themselves apart from their regular food because they wanted to set their heart, their mind, their strength on God. They were praying for God. The Holy Spirit spoke through a prophet of God "separate unto me Barnabus and Paul for the work of the ministry."

Barnabus was sent by the Church of Jerusalem. In this instance God was using the prophet to send Barnabus and Paul into missionary preaching together. In this instance God not only confirms the friendship of Barnabus and Paul but also their ministry together as a team. They were strengthened by each other; they were a good team. They went out doing the work of the ministry. They were planting churches. Often your close friends will be in some way connected to your ministry. I am not saying always, but often there will be people of like precious faith close to you and in some way connected in ministry.

I am not saying you can't have any non-Christian friends, but I am saying they shouldn't be in your innermost circle of friends. Your best friends should be Christians friends. If they are not, you pray that God would put godly friends into your life. God can bring the right people into your life that will encourage you and cause you to aim for excellence.

Paul the Encourager

The Apostle Paul was an encourager also. Paul encourages people throughout his books. He is a tremendous encourager; because he is such an excellent teacher, we often don't discuss him as an encourager. He is not only a teacher, an encourager but also a writer of scripture given by God. He wrote most of the New Testament. Read all his beginnings and endings of his books and he is so strong in encourager. Example in Timothy. 2 Thessalonians 3: 18 The grace of our Lord Jesus Christ be with you all. Amen.

We may think these are nice words almost like a hallmark card. But no, no no – he literally is speaking words of blessing to the saints. May the grace of Christ be with you. Do we encourage our friends when we are with them? I hope we do. We should speak scripture into their lives.

He encourages Timothy. O, it is so strong. We get to see him pouring his heart into Timothy as he is discipling and training him.

In 2 Timothy 1: 2-4 2 To Timothy, my beloved son:

1Grace, mercy, and peace, from God the Father and Christ Jesus our Lord.

He greets him with godly love not just a salutation. He sincerely imparts words of blessing. We should decide that when we shake someone's hand at church we mean the words we say – true impartation of blessing. He is saying that he is praying for him and it is a strong encouragement.

3 I thank God, whom I serve with a pure conscience as my forefathers did, as I continually remember you in my prayers night and day, 4 greatly desiring to see you, remembering your tears, that I may be filled with joy, 5 remembering the genuine faith that first lived in your grandmother Lois and your mother Eunice and that I am persuaded lives in you also.

He shares his heart full of love towards him. He is imparting his love and not just the love of A person but of someone who has mentored him and trained him up in the Christian faith and established him. The same heart is here in Philemon. This is one of the people he won to Christ while in prison.

Rejoicing in Others' Spiritual Growth

He appeals on behalf of Onesimus who he won to Christ. He disciple him and his bond with him is spiritual. Onesimus has been an encourager to Paul. A Christian who wins someone to Christ is encouraged by his disciples because as they grow in Christ, we are encouraged. Encouragers love to see someone they have encouraged and taught, rise up in the Christian faith. Many teachers as well are encouragers because they love to see the development in their students. Many pastors are encouragers. They love to see the congregation growing in faith.

If the faith level of everyone in the congregation would remain the same, the pastor would not be happy. The teacher would not be happy if the students graduated from the class with the exact information they knew before the class. The teacher is hoping to impart. The pastor is hoping to impart and they do it encouraging their students to learn. God gives them words of wisdom to encourage and advise the students and learners. God can give you wisdom to impart in people's lives.

Philemon

Vs 9 yet for love's sake I rather appeal to you—I, Paul, an old man, and now also a prisoner of Jesus Christ— 10 I appeal to you on behalf of my son Onesimus, whose father I have become in my imprisonment, 11 who in the past was unprofitable to you, but now he is profitable to you and to me.

In some way Onesimus did something wrong but Paul appeals so strongly that he says anything he owes you – I will give you myself. This is the ultimate encourager. He says Oneismus has been such a blessing to him that he would repay anything owed.

17 If then you consider me a partner, receive him as you would me. 18 If he wronged you or owes you anything, charge this to my account.

Personal Example

I can remember one person who was an usher in the church but he had a strong gift of encouragement. Our church started at 7pm so about 6pm, he would arrive at the church and greet every person he saw on the street. He would walk up and down the street (a large Church) around the church inviting people to church. If you were a Christian, he would shake your hand and encourage you. He never said God bless you without meaning it with all his being. He would glow with the joy of the LORD.

You would always smile and feel welcomed because of him. No one told him to do this activity of greeting people and inviting people to church. He just did it. He would encourage you. If you were a non-Christian, he would go walking alongside a person and start talking and witnessing about Jesus. He got many people to come to service that way. He got people to come to church who were not church people. He knew how to use his gift in the church and outside the church. You don't use the gifts exactly the same, but the same gifts can be used to build up the saints and also to bring people to Christ.

The peace that is on your life will be notable to non-Christians. They will know us as different because of the fruit of the Spirit in our lives. There is a place for using the encouraging gifts to each other in the Body of Christ and in Evangelism. There was another man I will speak of who walking around the corridors of the church and in the lobby. What he would do is walk around before the service in the church building. Any unrest of any type example a mother with small children, juggling kids and a diaper bag etc. he would go up alongside her and help her and bless them in the name of the LORD.

If he saw you walking in without a smile on your face, he would come right over to you. It was like a magnet. He would be attracted to you and begin to encourage you. The Lord would use him to speak words of encouragement to you. He would say so glad to see you or other welcoming words. He might pray for you there. Not in the sanctuary – before church in the hallway. He used every opportunity possible to encourage you. He was not appointed by the ministry of the church to do it – but he did it as a ministry. He believed the right thing to do. It was notable. Everybody knew him as a strong encourager.

God can use you to speak words of comfort, words of faith, words to strengthen to sisters and brothers by caring for them and comforting them. God may inspire you to give a solution to someone. If you are feeling the LORD lead you, go over an speak to the person. Encourage them. The more you obey those inner promptings from the LORD, the more God will use you. Start talking to them and maybe the person will reveal something to you and you can pray for them. Encouragers are required in the body of Christ.

7 MOTIVATION OF GIVING

In talking about the gift of giving, we are talking about physical substance of some type. Usually it means giving money. It could also be giving land or possessions such as cars or trucks or homes. A person motivated by giving, has this as a primary directive of his or her life. Givers choose to give as one of their goals for each day, month, year etc. How much can I give? This is what the person is thinking of mostly. How can I give? In what way can I give finances or resources to advance the gospel? How can I express the love of God in giving?

The motivation is spiritual. The person is prompted by the Holy Spirit to do it. It might be in an exact particular need such as purchasing a well in a third world nation for a village. It might be more general such as "start giving". The person would do research as to where to give financially. It might be to a missionary or evangelist. Certainly if you feel a prompting to give, you should directly give to those ministries that have blessed and do bless your life. But those motivated by giving do it in more ways: some give of their possessions, their time, their prayers etc.

All Christians have some gift of giving because it is a prime directive of a Christian to preach Christ or to finance others who preach Christ. The gift of giving lavishly is not as common in the majority of people. This gift of giving – the anointing on the giving could cause people to give their personal possessions such as their homes or automobiles for the furtherance of the gospel.

To know where the gift of giving comes from I will discuss the following:

John 3:16 "For God so loved the world that He gave His only begotten Son, that whoever believes in Him should not perish, but have eternal life. 17 For God did not send His Son into the world to condemn the world, but that the world through Him might be saved.

God Gave

This is essential to our Christian belief; receiving Jesus as our Saviour and LORD is accepting God's gift to us. If we do not receive, we cannot be

Christians. The motivation was He loved so He gave. He loved us so much with the agape (God kind) of unconditional love that He gave Jesus. Ever since man sinned, with Adam and Eve in the garden of Eden, God has been offering forgiveness through His covenants or promises to man. God has been the initiator of restoration.

God made a way for us to be restored in friendship, in closeness of relationship, to God.

I am not talking about regular Christian giving in this teaching. Regular Christian giving includes the tithe which is 10% of our income. I am talking about giving beyond the tithe. There are these usual Christian types of giving: tithes, offerings, alms, first fruits giving. All of these things may be included in the motivation of giving but I am not talking about normal, regular Christian giving; I am talking about that which stands out as more than usual, something that goes beyond all expectation.

Luke 6: 38 Give, and it will be given to you: Good measure, pressed down, shaken together, and running over will men give unto you. For with the measure you use, it will be measured unto you.

Giving and Receiving

What is it? God's principle is that if we give, it shall be given to us. It is a principle just as there are principles or laws of physics such as gravity, or properties of chemicals. The principle of giving and receiving is much the same. If we give, we shall receive. It most often is not from the place we give to. It comes from God who keeps nooks on our giving. He is the one that will cause a blessing to come to us from the source He chooses. It may be a supernatural sort of giving or it could be a gentle Holy Spirit prompting of giving. Giving (our part) releases a gift towards us (on God's part). As we give, it opens God's hand to bless us, for someone to give to us. God always gives to us more than what we gave. It may not be in the same way. He chooses the person and the way.

Some people actually believe it is like a pyramid scheme. You give and other people around you will give to you. They may believe that if you give $50.00, you should get an increase of so much. God most certainly can multiply our gift and always gives to us more than what we give, but there is more to it. Sometimes what we reap is not financial but in the area of our need. God always gives an abundance to us. God gives us more than what we could imagine. I am talking about blessings that are financial, physical and spiritual. I am saying it can affect any part of our lives. The blessings of the LORD are beyond what we can contain. He gives an overflow of goodness, of mercy, of favour to us.

The Principle of Giving

The principal is giving and receiving from God – He will always give to us. The true motivation of giver does not give to get. The giver gives because it is a spiritual gift which compels him or her to care for others by giving finances, resources etc. The principle is activated by our giving. It is always true, just as the fact you throw a ball, the principle of motion and thrust come into play. The person may be knowledgeable of it. We should certainly grasp and thank God for what is given to us. We should not be shy about receiving. It is God's pleasure to give to us and to bless us. The person with the sincere gift of giving isn't trying to get more from God. They are trying to give because the love of God within them compels them to give to advance the gospel.

The Main Drive

How can I give to build churches? How can I give to build Christian schools and Bible colleges? How can I send Evangelists who will go to countries I can't go to right now – knowing they will share Christ with those people? How can I give so the gospel will be preached on TV, on radio, through the media that can be used – how can I give so it is used to promote the gospel of Jesus Christ? The person is motivated by how can I give. Their motive is to spread the gospel and their way is to use what they have to do it.

The heart attitude matters to God. If you are giving for any other motive, God knows. God sees not only your giving but the motive for your giving. The Pharisees would keep the Levitical laws that commanded us to give by blowing a trumpet and announcing they were giving to fulfill the laws of Moses. They gave so they could receive the recognition of men.

It is true that when someone gives a large amount of money or resources that the public will congratulate and thank them publically: often with plaques, cornerstones on buildings or naming the buildings after them. A person motivated by giving will run from those types of situation. They are more likely to make the person or people promise not to announce the gift unless it is to motivate others to give match funding.

Giving to impress others should never be our motivation. It is soulish, sensual and devilish. Boasting in our giving is not good. If we give for wrong motives, we will not receive a heavenly reward. God rewards the cheerful giver: one with pure motives.

Matthew 6:
6 Be sure that you not do your charitable deeds before men to be seen by them. Otherwise you have no reward from your Father who is in heaven.

2 Therefore, when you do your charitable deeds, do not sound a trumpet before you as the hypocrites do in the synagogues and in the streets, that they may be honored by men. Truly I say to you, they have their reward. 3 But when you do your charitable deeds, do not let your left hand know what your right hand is doing, 4 that your charitable deeds may be in secret. And your Father who sees in secret will Himself reward you openly.

The Giver Receives

The other way to see this scripture is that if you are giving with a pure motive, you most certainly are receiving a heavenly reward. The scripture above means that we should give with simplicity and with true motive. This type of giving is always honourable to God. It is not seeking and earthly reward from people. It is obeying the prompting of the Holy Spirit to give. It is obeying the LORD's leading.

In the last century, what has developed in the Christian world that if someone gives, the organization or charity gives them something. It could be a CD of the month; it could be a sculpture or a painting etc. I'm not saying it is wrong to give something to our partners. Those ministries I support often give something to their partners. They are sowing into our lives. They view it is such. It is not like a transaction of finances for goods. It is a sowing back into our lives. They literally believe the gift they send is a token of how God will bless us. If we only give to get – it is not the motivation of giving. A person motivated by giving may give to someone who could never repay him or her.

Romans 12: 8 he who exhorts, in exhortation; he who gives, with generosity; he who rules, with diligence; he who shows mercy, with cheerfulness.
Motive

We are to give with simplicity. We are to give as unto God Himself. It is right to respect those who give. We should thank God for them and pray for them. You will notice in the book of Acts that all the Jewish people knew that Cornelius had given finances to build a synagogue. He was highly esteemed for this tremendous gift. Believe me, if a Roman centurion was giving to a Jewish cause, he was not publicly announcing it. He was doing it in secret. Somehow the people found out. We should give with a humble heart. If we are proud or boastful it is the opposite of what God requires. Our motive should be love for God.

Mary of Bethany

In Matthew 26 an example of lavish giving is shown in Mary of Bethany. She gives the most precious thing she had. She comes to Jesus and pours it on Jesus. Judas believes it has been wasted and says in covetous anger it could have been used for the poor – but really he was a thief even though he was trusted with the treasury.

John 12 : 4 But one of His disciples, Judas Iscariot, Simon's son, who would betray Him, said, 5 "Why was this ointment not sold for three hundred denarii[b] and given to the poor?" 6 He said this, not because he cared for the poor, but because he was a thief. And having the money box, he used to steal what was put in it.

It seems like a waste to those who would have used it differently. The woman who gave the gift lavished it on Jesus knowing He was the most important part of her life. Jesus does not reprove her gift but says she has done it as an anointing for his burial. The person motivated to give is obeying the prompting of the LORD to give, Others may not understand why the gift was given. Others may see it as being a waste. Mary was giving in an act of worship, the most precious thing she had. The motivation of giving can be credited as part of our spiritual worship.

Mary of Bethany has spiritual significance. First of all, she is giving all that she has. It is most precious to her. If you live to please people, you will never be happy because no one will understand why you are giving. Only those with the motivation of giving, or those who get a revelation from the LORD will understand your giving.

Luke 8: 2 and some women who had been healed of evil spirits and infirmities: Mary, called Magdalene, from whom seven demons had come out, 3 and Joanna, the wife of Chuza, Herod's steward, and Susanna, and many others, who supported Him with their possessions.

Women are mentioned as among those who contributed to Jesus' ministry financially. They had been healed, delivered, set free by Jesus. Please know that in their society women were not treated as equals. For them to be mentioned at all in the scriptures is peculiar and shows that God cared about their giving as it is memorialized through the scripture. Their giving unto Jesus was noteworthy. God cared about their giving and included it to show us He sees and cares about the givers, It also shows us Jesus and His disciples welcomed women as co-labourers in the gospel.

In 1 Corinthians 13: 3 If I give all my goods to feed the poor, and if I give my body to be burned, and have not love, it profits me nothing.

We are taught about love in this chapter. It is known as the love chapter. If we are not giving with the motivation of love, we are not giving with a right heart. Giving is not only in the New Testament; it was commanded by God that we care for the poor.

In Leviticus 19: 9 When you reap the harvest of your land, you shall not reap up to the edge of your field, nor shall you gather the gleanings of your harvest. 10 You shall not glean bare your vineyard, nor shall you gather every fallen grape of your vineyard. You shall leave them for the poor and stranger: I am the Lord your God.

Giving to Those Who Can Never Repay

We are taught about always leaving something for the poor. They were not to pick all the fruit; they were not to glean all their fields but to leave the corners on purpose for those who had nothing. They were not only to care for their own poor but also for any strangers that might have a need. God promises to bless them for giving to the poor; God is the defender of the widow and the orphan. They did not have a health care system like we do – leaving something for those who had nothing was a direct way of caring for the poor, widows, orphans etc.

We should be giving to the poor in remembrance of how God has blessed us and prospered us.

The Tabernacle

In Exodus 36, there is a teaching on the Tabernacle and how God instructed Moses to build it. This is not a teaching on the tabernacle, but God did give specific instruction to Moses how to build it; it was the place for worship and how worship would be conducted on the earth; God established it. Jewish people didn't make up a way to worship God. No, no, no. God dictated to Moses how they would worship, what would please Him. There is no part of the Old Testament worship that does not have spiritual significance to us in the New Testament.

Designed by God

God gave the design. God gave the instruction for the order of sacrifice and offerings. It is God's instruction to us. God gifted the craftsmen to follow the designs that God gave them to build the various things to be used in worship. They were artists, carvers, silversmiths, goldsmiths, artisans, sowing fabrics… all types of intricate, complex, skills and craftsmen. These are the types of people God used to build the tabernacle.

The People Gave Their Best

Exodus 36: 3 They received from Moses all the offerings which the children of Israel had brought to do the work of the service of the sanctuary, and they continued to bring to him freewill offerings every morning. 4 And all the skilled men who were doing all the work of the sanctuary came from the work they were doing,

They gave the most precious things they had; they gave their talents as well as their substance. Because God was the designer and project manager of the job, every physical need was met so that there was an abundance. They literally gave so much, Moses had to instruct the people not to give any more. People wanted to serve the LORD, so it was their honour to do it unto God – so the need was met and more than enough was collected. The people had a willing heart.

I've been a part of several churches that were involved in huge building projects. It meant the doubling of our sanctuary; more land, much money and also the giving of people's time as volunteers in many areas around the church. I have seen and been a part of giving personal bests in finances and in volunteering. It is exciting to be building a sanctuary for God.

Finally, more than enough had been given and they asked Moses to tell the people they didn't have to give any more. Exodus 36: 5 and they said to Moses, "The people are bringing much more than is needed for the service of the work which the Lord commanded us to do.

More than Enough

If you are in ministry and you are raising finances for a project, be honest with the people. Once the need has been met, thank them and inform them that need was fulfilled. It is so important but rarely done by preachers today. It causes the people to feel a sense of accomplishment to know their contribution helped to accomplish something for God. You can always start a new project or new campaign. Giving regular reports as to where the finances or gifts is going boosts the spirits of the givers. Givers like to meet needs. They want to see something accomplished for God.

Giving a Report

If you are in ministry, God will always give you projects to accomplish for His glory. There is the building of churches, Christian schools, Bible colleges, training and vocational centers where the people can be trained. There are so many worthy projects, but the people will not know they are making a difference unless you show them where their money is going. It should either be done project by project or by regular reports on giving and what has been accomplished by the donations and how a dollar gift contributed to the projects thus far.

I am saying it makes a difference to the people's morale. They believe they are making a difference because they are seeing the results. Also, it shows that you are publicly thanking God for what has been accomplished through your ministry. If you invite people to give in a public way, thank them in a public way and show them the results. Take photos or movies showing what their donations or partnerships have done. This is accountability that not only keeps the standards of government but surpasses them by showing the people specifically the spending.

On the earth, there were always be some poor people, until Jesus comes to earth and establishes His throne in Jerusalem. It means we should be kind and caring and giving to those who do not have essential things that we have an abundance of such as money, food, clothing etc. we should be merciful. Those of us who did not grow up wealthy should also remember the way God. provided for us – often with people giving to us. We should want to care that people's needs are met.

In John 19, we have an example of extravagant giving; it is after Jesus' death. It is Joseph of Arimathea who was a Pharisee, who was Jesus' uncle (other texts inform us) goes to Pilot to beg for the body of Jesus. He offers to give his own tomb. He does it secretly because he would have been persecuted or even killed for associating with Jesus.

John 19: 38 After this, Joseph of Arimathea, being a disciple of Jesus, but secretly for fear of the Jews, asked Pilate that he might take away the body of Jesus. Pilate gave him permission. So he came and took away His body.

I am all in favour of being public about our Christian faith. There are so many examples of Christians who had to hide their faith or risk death. Even today in many countries, there are Christians martyred or imprisoned for their faith. There are people in the Bible who confessed they believed in God but also asked mercy that in front of their master, they had to show respect for a different God. This is hard for us to grasp in our culture. I am not advocating it, but we should be merciful to those who cannot publicly show their faith. There are people all over the earth who cannot publicly give to the gospel; they do it in secret. They worship in secret because they will be martyred.

Giving Extravagantly

Joseph of Arimathea gives his own physical tomb. He takes the body of Jesus and Nicodemus, also a Pharisee who Jesus actually won to the LORD. When Jesus spoke to him, it touched his heart and life. Somehow he understood that Jesus was the Messiah. It wasn't a public funeral – but it was a lavish gift. It included all the oils and spices to be used. He gave his best. It is quite a large gift, giving of your own burial place, giving of what is necessary for burial. These people knew that if would have been found out, they would have received punishment or death. Jesus was considered a criminal. This is lavish giving; it is also secret giving.

There was such a love among the Christians that they shared together, had communion together and even gave of their property and possessions so that those Christians who had nothing received something. They cared about each other.

Acts 2: 44 All who believed were together and had all things in common. 45 They sold their property and goods and distributed them to all, according to their need.

A specific example of this is seen in Acts with Barnabas.

Acts 4: 36 Joseph, whom the apostles called Barnabas (which means, Son of Encouragement), a Levite from the land of Cyprus, 37 sold a field he owned, and brought the money and placed it at the apostles' feet.

Caring for Christians

Once I became a Christian, I started loving the people around me. I cared about the Christians in my church and also those in the global church. I was a student so I didn't have much extra but I had some. I would care that those who had nothing with food or clothes or whatever. Mostly it was small things; the price was not expensive – but I gave up extra money and sometimes sacrificed to do it. Only God know but He always blessed me in some way for doing it. God supplied and on several occasions used other Christians to give to me – without me asking. It was God nudging the person to give.

If we are in unity, in singleness of heart, we will care about each other. We will live in fervency and zeal. Miracles, signs, wonders will follow us if we are in singleness of heart. Giving was a sign of the love they had for each other. Do we care for others in our church? Do we care about the poor or those who have nothing? We should be the givers. We should be the leaders who host events for people who do not know Christ. We should include a dinner or some kind or refreshments. We should have a food bank or clothing donation drive. We should be leaders in caring about others.

The Church Should Give

We as a church should meet the needs of those within the church. I mean this at a basic level of food and clothing but also if we own a company, and we know someone needs a job and we can hire, we should consider hiring people from within our church. We should invest in our own people. If we could host training sessions or help to give someone a trade, we should care enough to do it. Not only caring to meet the immediate needs, we should invest our time and our talents to train up others.

Do we have someone to give to that we know will use it wisely to meet the needs of people? I'm not speaking so much of an organization. Is there an apostle in your life that you know will care for others? It could be through your church or through a parachurch ministry. You recognize the authority on the person to care for the corporate church.

Modern Day Apostle Lester Sumrall

I remember an awesome meeting in Detroit with Lester Sumrall. He was in his late 70's or early 80's but he was still globetrotting around the world preaching the gospel discipling, training and outrunning other pastors and ministers. He was so trusted by God by God imparting his heart to him that he could convey it to masses of people. He was a faithful pastor and missionary and evangelist. He was a mighty man of faith; what I remember most about him was his authority as an Apostle.

While he was in Jerusalem, God spoke to him most seriously about His soon coming. He also said that there were literally thousands of Christians in Africa who were praying for answers and for daily needs but they were dying. The main reason for this was because the Christians in countries that had finances were not caring for our sisters and brothers in other nations. He explained that God revealed to him if we Christians would fast several times a week and give the money to world missions instead of using it ourselves, thousands of Christians could be fed.

LeSea Ministries is known for giving to the poor. The biggest expense in getting food and clothing to those in Africa is the cost of shipping. Lester Sumrall said he would obey God's instruction. A huge US bomber was donated to his ministry. With that bomber that had been transformed to a cargo plane and a huge ship with large cargo bays, LeSea began missionary deliveries of rice, corn and other grains to Africa.

As Pastor Sumrall had been in ministry more than 40 years, he had established a reputation of honesty and integrity. He was given special huge donations from companies. For example, a ship full of Rice Crispies. Literally huge corporations donated food for this worthy cause. As Lester Sumrall explained this charge from the LORD (for Christians that have food and clothing to give to those who have not) , the Pastor of the large church stepped forward to announce his church would cover so many thousand people; all over the congregation, people stood to volunteer to give towards this ministry of helping other Christians we may never meet on the earth. They were giving to the Apostle because we all knew that he wasn't in it for any other reason than obeying God and caring for our brothers and sisters in Africa.

Accountability

We the church need to know that the money is going to where we are intending it to go. Oh Please take note; there are many reputable Christian ministries that do exactly what they say they will do about caring for the poor or needy. This is not instead of the gospel; it accompanies the gospel. We should care for the natural needs of those who can never repay us – Christian charity.

Don't give blindly; don't give to anyone that asks; I'm saying give as the Lord leads you to reputable Christians who are faithful to keep their word.

Givers Motivate Others to Give

In situations like the one I described, givers will often give a large amount of money promising to match the gifts of others; example if people give $1, 000.- they will give $1,000. Givers don't want to boast their giving but if their giving can in some way lead to others giving, they will give to motivate others. It's not about just raising money; it is giving so more can be done for the gospel. The more people who receive from the giving to the gospel, the more thanksgiving rises up to God. Your giving, can release thanksgiving to someone on the other side of the giving.

King David an Extravagant Giver

2 Samuel 6

King David is someone known for extravagant giving to God. First of all, please know he gathered together over 30, 000 worshippers. He reinstated the praise and worship in the Tabernacle. He instituted praise and worship and prayer. As David brought the Ark of God to Jerusalem, which contained the Holy Presence of God, he danced and sang with the worshipping priests. This was the same Ark that Moses built according to God's design. It was a box that had a seat on top with angels whose wings spread over the mercy seat. It contained, as God instructed, the commandments as given to Moses, the rod of Aaron that budded and some manna.

They were not instructed to open the Ark and it was forbidden for them to touch the Ark.

Once the Ark had been captured from Israel, there was sorrow. The Ark was not only the presence of God that gave them a focus of worship, but it was a sign of their loss of the most precious part of Israel – God. Once the Ark was recovered, David was rejoicing with all his might. The Levitical priests leading the parade of worshippers were dancing, playing instruments, worshipping God for the restoration of worship with the Ark of God.

They sang and danced rejoicing that the presence of God was being returned to the people of God. David was a king; he could have ridden on a throne born by his servants. He could have ridden a horse. He chose to be with the priests, walking, worshipping and dancing with all his might. This parade was for the glory of God. David was a worshipper.

2 Samuel 6: 17 They brought the ark of the Lord and set it in its place inside the tent that David had erected for it. Then David offered burnt offerings and peace offerings before the Lord. 18 When David had finished offering the burnt offerings and peace offerings, he blessed the people before the Lord of Hosts. 19 He distributed to all of the people, the entire multitude of Israel, both men and women, one bread cake, one date cake, and one raisin cake to each one. Then all of the people left, each to his house

The Ark was placed in a proper spot. He paid for sacrifices and offerings to be give. Thousands of animals were offered in thanksgiving. He followed the words instructed by Moses. Then he gave extravagantly more. He gave all the people who gathered to watch the parade, over 30, 000 people, a cake of bread, a piece of meet and a flagon of wine. Why did he do it? He was celebrating the return of the Ark and he wanted the people to be rejoicing and thanking God for the return of the Ark. It was significant. He wanted others to glorify God.

Giving Releases Thanksgiving

2 Corinthians 9: 7 Let every man give according to the purposes in his heart, not grudgingly or out of necessity, for God loves a cheerful giver. 8 God is able to make all grace abound toward you, so that you, always having enough of everything, may abound to every good work. 9 As it is written:

"He has dispersed abroad, He has given to the poor;
    His righteousness remains forever."[a]

10 Now He who supplies seed to the sower and supplies bread for your food will also multiply your seed sown and increase the fruits of your righteousness. 11 So you will be enriched in everything to all bountifulness, which makes us give thanks to God.

12 For the administration of this service not only supplies the need of the saints, but is abundant also through many thanksgivings to God.

Giving With a Right Heart

Give expecting the glory of God to manifest. It has spiritual significance as well as meeting a physical need. We need to preach with boldness that giving is to be an act of worship. It says God rejoices at a joyful giver. If you would give but do it be grudgingly, don't give; you cannot be blessed with that heart attitude. Finances are always an issue to people because it is of your substance – its part of your identity, who you are.

If you are giving with a pure heart, it touches the core of your being. Oh there are blessings upon you. People have selfish motives don't give with a pure heart. If you give only to get, the motive isn't right. If you have a hard heart about giving, you should pray and ask God to forgive you and heal you. A person motivated by giving, gives joyfully, for the glory of God, to release thanksgiving in the earth.

We are Christians, we should be giving to our local church. There are ministries that bless us, we should be giving to them. We are to honour those who give to us spiritually. Your spirit will want to respond to the minsters who feed us spiritually. Don't believe the lie all they want is your money.

A Miserly Spirit

Money is necessary for the gospel to be preached. Books, CDs, DVDs, broadcasting, giving clothing or food – all requires money. There are reputable people who receive your money to give to the gospel. They do what they promise. Some Christians miss being blessed by giving because they only complain about the money that goes into ministry. There are huge department stores and banks, and services. All of the commercial realm on earth wants your money. That is what we use on earth to do transactions. If there is any part of you that believes the church should not be collecting money for projects to help people, repent and ask God to forgive you. Get that miserly spirit out of you.

We should be known for our giving. People should want to know why we are giving so much so that the answer would automatically arise, Oh don't you know – those are Christians; they are always giving. God is the one who blesses you. He is going to bless you no matter what. He is your source – not a person or a place – God will bless you because He wants to bless you so that you can give more. God is the origin of the blessing upon our lives. We are blessed by the LORD so we can be a blessing to others.

Givers in North America

We in North America are wealthy compared to most people on the planet. I know there are poor people here, but in many countries, there is no health care; in many countries, there is no free education. We have government assistance for people that have no job or way for a job. I thank God we care for those within our country. By no means can a person live a high life on government assistance. It barely covers the minimum necessities. We as Christians could make a difference in their lives through volunteering and through giving.

I am not promoting communism. I am promoting giving – to care for other people. First we want to share the gospel with them, but how could we preach Christ to them and believe we are right with God if we don't care they don't have basic necessities? May God give you a willingness in heart to give to the gospel. Giving is a fruit of righteousness. It comes from a living right spirit. It produces spiritual fruit not only natural fruit. Give as the LORD directs you. Obey the promptings of the Holy Spirit to give; you can never out give God.

8 MOTIVATION OF LEADERSHIP

In motivational gifts such as serving or mercy, there is a large percentage of Christians who have them. Leadership or ruling does not include many people with this motivation. The reason is because the Body of Christ doesn't need as many. The body of Christ is like a human body; there are no extra parts. Every part has a function. They used to actually believe that the appendix was an extra part but they found out it that it serves a purpose.

There is a need for leadership and leaders but not as much as the other giftings. As I've said, there is some of each of the giftings in all of us because Christ lives in us. Those who are called to be leaders may be Apostles, Prophets, Evangelists, pastors or teachers. They could also serve in other ministries within the church or also be leaders in their careers.

Visionaries

God raises up the rulers or those with the motivation of Leadership, and He does it in different ways. These people are able to see an overall picture. They can visualize how to organize and successfully complete a task or host an event. They can see possibilities in situations where others are not. They are able to actualize and rally support for the performance of something.

This is a supernatural gift. I am not just speaking of a natural ability to lead. In this capacity, the leader will be impressed by God of certain things that should be done. It could be the building of a church or Christian school or Bible college. It could be the start of a new ministry or service for our church or a new outreach center to ministry to the community.

Unique Visions

For instance, Pastor Bill Winston and his congregation purchased a shopping mall and it is used as a church and ministry center. Another example would be Pastor Matthew Barnett who purchased a huge building and uses it as a church, recovery ministry and outreach center in Los Angeles. I am talking about visionaries who see potential beyond the scope of what most people would think. These leaders not only see the vision, but they can motivate people to give and to care about the vision and take a place within it. Not all leaders are in that category but some are. Some pastors are focused on their local church. Others may impact the province or state or the nation or the earth. Leaders have various levels of anointing – or abilities given directly by God for the purposes of building up, encouraging, establishing the Body of Christ.

They not only see how it can but done, but also how it can be organized. They can arrange people with resources to accomplish goals. That's pretty amazing. I am saying the person is able to see the thing before it exists, what is required to perform it, and how to organize the people to do it. The leader can literally spot giftings in people. They are given insight by God to help them in directing the people and helping them to grow by using them. They encourage people and give them opportunities to use their gifts in the church. They can also coordinate people with resources. People put their trust in them.

Givers in the Early Church

In the book of Acts 4, people actually were moved with compassion towards those in the church and they sold extra property and things they had and donated large sums of money to the Apostles so that Christians who had no food did not go without. God moved on their hearts to give. The Apostles were chosen by Jesus to be the foundation of his Church. They were able to see the manifestations of God's glory on people and assign people to tasks for a common purpose.

People literally trusted the Apostles with their finances and resources. Leaders are able to raise the funding necessary for a project. God gives them the vision but also the way to impart the vision so that others care about it. Because they are often Charismatic, spiritually as well as attractors of people, they are held to a different standard by God. The scriptures describing the godly character show God's priorities for character and integrity stronger than an emphasis on giftings.

1 Timothy 3: 3 This is a faithful saying: If a man desires the office of an overseer, he desires a good work. 2 An overseer then must be blameless, the husband of one wife, sober, self-controlled, respectable, hospitable, able to teach; 3 not given to drunkenness, not violent, not greedy for money, but patient, not argumentative, not covetous; 4 and one who manages his own house well, having his children in submission with all reverence. 5 For if a man does not know how to manage his own house, how will he take care of the church of God? 6 He must not be newly converted, so that he does not become prideful and fall into the condemnation of the devil.

Leaders as Standard Bearers

Leaders must set a standard for the Body of Christ. They must have these qualities so that they can be as examples to others. Hospitality means more than inviting people to your home. It can mean generosity, inviting people to gatherings outside of the home. It has to do with being a friendly and warm person who can inspire others to be welcoming and involved. They teach, disciple, share, talk on a spiritual level etc. Please see these are the criteria for us to use when choosing a leader. It doesn't mean that can't use someone from outside this description; He can and He does.

Leaders should be known as of a good reputation within the church and also in the community. They are respected by even those of different faith because of the qualities they display. They should be people who can give their word and who will perform it. These people should not be covetous or drunkards. Literally God want His people alert and sincere.

Leaders can attract all sorts of people. They attract people who are not only the same as them but also those very different. They have a charisma that is God- given. People like them. Christians will like them but so will others. They should be careful in conduct because of the numbers of people affected and influenced by them. They are gifted to see people's giftings and they must not manipulate their influence to persuade people into doing wrong things or misusing their authority to abuse or use people. They may be able to see potential in areas they themselves should not be a part of. Example, they have the ability to see what could be – but they should pray about it to see if God wants them to go in that direction.

If the leader simply sees and does but does not pray about God's will, it is possible he or she can get into areas that will ultimately lead them away from their purposes and main priorities. It can lead to a waste of resources, people and time. The leader must be accountable to God. As all of us must seek God's will, the leader is not exempt. Only with the anointing of the LORD on the leader can the leader properly glorify God. This requires connection with God and following the will of the LORD. There have been stories of leaders who believe it is a good idea to start something new and they do and it fails because the leader did not seek the LORD. They can see potential but that doesn't immediately mean they are the ones to bring it into being.

Spirit Lead Visionary

The visionary gifting can be beyond what you presently are able to do. For instance, you may have the vision for it and you are the right person but it isn't the right time for you to do it. There are so many people in our culture that want to make you into a superstar. You must be careful to be led by the Holy Spirit and not by the people around you. They will try to slick talk you into going beyond what you know. They will brand you, give you a media identity, sell you and package you to the media so that you will have mass appeal. If you believe the lie of what they create, it can mess up your life. It can lead to idol worship, sin, corruption etc.

The person in leadership should always consider God as the first choice for wise counsel. There are people who would like to promote you but those people might not be sent by God. There is a sobriety in this or a warning to be prayerful no matter what your motivational gift is. We should not accept every opportunity even though it seems exciting or something we would like to do. I want to give you the image of a carnival. There are rides; there are games; there are masses of people; each booth entices you to come do it. Some people are drawn into each one. I am saying the leader gets more of these types of opportunities in his or her life and they must prayerfully consider their steps and the consequences.

Influence

If a leader goes astray or sins, he or she may influence hundreds or thousands of lives. I am not talking about a slight inconvenience. They are like a spiritual covering over the people they shepherd. Those people will be left without protection or care. Some of them will wander. I wish I could say I do not know what it is like, but I have seen the devastation a fallen leader brings to not only the local church but all of those who were in his or her life. The media zooms in on those situations and people who have never met the leader have a negative view of his or her and also Christians. The leader always sets an example, by his or her obedience to God or the opposite. It matters not only for us but for hundreds or thousands of people affected by our decisions.

More than once, their families are mentioned. The leaders should have one spouse. Their relationship should be good. They should agree in ministry decisions. There should be harmony in their home. Their children should be models of proper Christian living. I am not stereo typing this – I am referring to the scripture. The parents invest in their children and teach them and use them in ministry with them. The character – God develops it.

The care and teaching of the children are their responsibility. Some families will all be spiritual leaders, as with the Levitical priests.

Exodus

We would all like to be chosen in this manner. If we are going to be chosen for leadership, we would like it to be this way. Instead of wondering is God choosing me for leadership…we would like to know that we know the LORD has called us. In Exodus 3, Moses was living with Jethro and his family in Midian. He became a shepherd. He noticed the light on the mountain – it was a bush that appeared to be burning but didn't burn out. It caught his attention and he climbed the mountain to see why it was this way. It was unusual. It got his attention.

He was leading sheep, literally and he had a good life in Midian. He was a shepherd for 40 years after he was banished from Egypt. He had a wife and children and he was doing well. God knew how to get his attention. That burning bush attracts him. Moses climbs the mountain to see the bush. God literally called him by name "|Moses" and Moses answered.

Literally God spoke to him from a burning bush saying I am the God of Abraham. Literally Moses had a supernatural encounter with God, heard an audible voice. That's kind of the best way to get called. He knows directly from face to face conversation with God that God chose him. God talks first; he explained to Moses, what He wanted to do concerning delivering the people of Israel out of Egypt. God had developed Moses' character through his life experiences and all of his education and training, and life experience was actually for this day and the days that would follow. He was a person that God could share His heart with. God shares with Moses that He cares about His people.

Exodus 3: 10 Come now therefore, and I will send you to Pharaoh so that you may bring forth My people, the children of Israel, out of Egypt."

11 Moses said to God, "Who am I that I should go to Pharaoh and that I should bring forth the children of Israel out of Egypt?"

12 And He said, "Certainly I will be with you, and this will be a sign to you, that I have sent you: When you have brought forth the people out of Egypt, all of you shall serve God on this mountain."

This has got to be the most awesome way to get called into ministry. There is no question in Moses mind that it was God speaking to him, yet Moses still didn't believe he could do it. He tried to excuse himself by telling God he was weak. God reassured Him and spoke confidence into Him and instructed him to bring the people to worship on the mountain. Moses had questions. Rather than simply taking God at His word, he considered all the practical aspects. He tried to plead ignorance or inability but God reassured him and even allowed him to get Aaron to help him. He apologized to God for not being able to speak well. Moses was a humble man. In a different scripture it says He was the meekest man on the earth (Numbers 12: 3). He knew that if 2 million people were coming out of Egypt, out of slavery, it would have to be by God and not by his own hand.

1 Samuel 16

This is the choosing of David to be King over Israel by the Prophet Samuel as he is led by God. God directed Samuel to the home of David and to his family. They did not have the Holy Spirit residing in them in that day; they only had the Spirit come upon them. Samuel didn't know exactly who the LORD would choose until he got there. He saw the different sons and thought to himself who would seem to be the best leader? Several sons Samuel would have chosen, but God said no. God corrects him.

1 Samuel 16: 7 But the Lord said to Samuel, "Do not look on his appearance or on the height of his stature, because I have rejected him. For the Lord sees not as man sees. For man looks on the outward appearance, but the Lord looks on the heart."

The Choosing of a Leader

Don't choose someone to be your leader because he or she looks good. Is he or she proven? Is he or she chosen by God? Samuel prayerfully considers each of the sons of Jesse but does not find the one the LORD had chosen. Finally, David comes in; he had been tending the sheep. Samuel sees him.

1 Samuel 16: 7 12 So he sent and brought him in. Now he was ruddy with beautiful eyes and a good appearance. And the Lord said, "Arise, anoint him, for this is he."

Samuel obeyed and anointed David with a horn of anointing oil and prophesied that God chose him to be the next king of Israel. Samuel waited for God's word before he anointed the king. He chose what God chose. He was the youngest in the family, but he was chosen by God. Samuel faithfully spoke the will of the LORD.

The Making of a Leader

Notice that after this was done, Samuel left. The prophecy was not immediately fulfilled. It was years later before he became King. David was still a shepherd. Moses had been prophesied to be the deliverer of Israel but it does not manifest in his life until he was 80 years old. It is different than the calling of Moses in this way. After God spoke to Moses, He immediately sent Moses to get Aaron and to go to Egypt. Each calling of a leader is different. God will give instructions to the person that are unique to his or her life. Sometimes the calling of God could come on a person's life but there may be time that passes before the person is released into ministry. During this time, the person is doing some learning; God is developing character in him/ her.

The making of a leader by God is as though a potter (an artist who makes vessels from clay) is making a special vessel that is perfect for the opportunity he or she will be appointed for. Literally the lump of clay is placed on a potter's wheel and the clay is molded by the person's hands placing it in different areas on the clay. The sculpting of the shape is made by the person's hands and the shaping of the clay by the hands. I am saying that God does that with a person's character and development of talents and qualities. Leaders lives are more than a series of events. They are to learn through their experiences to help others and teach others.

Apostles and Prophets

There are Apostles and Prophets in the book of Acts and today who could release giftings and callings in people's lives. It is part of their job or their ministry.

A different type of calling to leadership is shown in the book of Acts. It is the most usual way leaders are chosen by people. They examined the character of certain people and prayed about it. Some churches take votes on it. They do something we usually don't do is that they cast lots which means they chose a name from a bunch of names like choosing a winner in the lottery. In Acts 2, the disciples decided to replace Judas because Judas betrayed Jesus and hung himself. They did the process above and chose Matthias.

Acts 1: 24 Then they prayed, "You, Lord, who knows the hearts of all men, show which of these two You have chosen 25 to take the place in this ministry and apostleship, from which Judas by transgression fell, to go to his own place." 26 Then they cast lots, and the lot fell on Matthias. So he was numbered with the eleven apostles.

Sometimes leaders are directly chosen by God as with the separation of Paul and Barnabus for ministry. Sometimes men choose who best fits the qualifications in scripture. Sometimes they are voted for by prayerful people who choose who they believe is the best person.

The Emergence of a Leader

In Acts 2 Peter arises as a leader in the Christian Church. They were waiting in the upper room for Jesus' promise of the Holy Spirit. The Holy Spirit comes upon them so mightily that it compels them to go into the streets and they are worshipping God in different languages of the pilgrims who have come to worship at Jerusalem for the Feast of Pentecost. Most of the people were thinking that is was amazing they were speaking the other languages without having studied them. Some people accused them of being drunk. They were attributing something of the Holy Spirit to something fleshly. Peter immediately stands up in defense of the Holy Spirit. He also takes the moment to teach the scriptural meaning.

Acts 2: 15 For these are not drunk, as you suppose, since it is the third hour of the day. 16 But this is what was spoken by the prophet Joel:

17 'In the last days it shall be,' says God,
     'that I will pour out My Spirit on all flesh;
your sons and your daughters shall prophesy,
     your young men shall see visions,
     and your old men shall dream dreams

Peter rose to the occasion; he could not let the accusation of them being drunk stay uncontested. He preaches his first Spirit filled sermon, with over 3, 000 people coming to Christ because of it. The Church of Jerusalem multiplies exponentially because of his prompting to teach the meaning of what is occurring. A leader will often feel a prompting to bring order or clarity to a situation where there is no leader. The person will feel a strong desire to do it. When a leader rises to the occasion, Oh there are so many people on the other side of that opportunity. The destiny of many people is affected by a leader's obedience or lack of it.

Raising up leaders is not something we should take lightly in the

Christian Church. We shouldn't vote for them because of outward things. If you are going to vote for a leader, let the Holy Spirit lead you and direct you, Line up that person with the scriptures. Where does that person stand?

A True Shepherd

Jesus teaches there is a correct way and a wrong way to be a leader. He teaches the difference between a true shepherd or a thief or hireling.

John 10 "Truly, truly I say to you, he who does not enter by the door into the sheepfold, but climbs up some other way, is a thief and a robber. 2 But he who enters by the door is the shepherd of the sheep. 3 To him the doorkeeper opens, and the sheep hear his voice. He calls his own sheep by name, and he leads them out. 4 When he brings out his own sheep, he goes before them. And the sheep follow him, for they know his voice. 5 Yet they will never follow a stranger, but will run away from him. For they do not know the voice of strangers."

There was a sheep pen with usually three sides around it and one side with a gate to the pen. The shepherd would guard over that area at night because wolves or wild animals would try to come and kill the sheep. The shepherd would go in by that door because the shepherd wasn't stealing. He had boldness to use the correct entrance. The shepherd was there to care for the sheep, to lead the sheep etc.

The shepherd came in the right way. It says his sheep know his voice. He talks to them and comforts them with his words. The shepherd knows the sheep and the sheep know the shepherd. They spend time together. This is also true of a leader. You know you have the right leader when you know his or her voice and it comforts you and feeds you. The shepherd actually fights against any enemies of the sheep; he or she would risk his or her life for the sheep. A thief would try to get in some other way. A hireling will not stay. If someone is a paid for pastor only because of the money or the opportunity, he or she will not feel the bond with the sheep. If the person is not a true shepherd, he or she will never risk his or her life for the sheep.

If the pastor only does the job for money, or for prestige or for any other reason than being lead by God, that person is really a hireling. I would compare it to the difference between a wife and a prostitute. The true pastor's heart is so closely knit to the sheep they are his or her main concern while he or she is with them and even during the week. God will place people on their hearts to pray for or visit or whatever. It is a supernatural relationship. The hireling will be like a wolf – may harm the sheep, may use the sheep, may beat the sheep or any other type of abuse. They will not care about the sheep.

God's Warning to False Leaders

God warns us of these types of shepherds in Ezekiel 34, the ones who don`t care for the sheep. They feed themselves with the best rather than care for the sheep first. It doesn`t mean they may not have gifts from God. Because of these gifts, they may become popular or famous. They will be able to see visions and gather money and resources. The difference is they are self-motivated. They are not lead by God`s Spirit. They may start schemes to get money from the people such as pyramid schemes or land schemes. They win the trust of the people and abuse that trust by stealing from the sheep. It is so important for the leader to be directed by God rather than his or her own self-motivation. If money is the motivator, it is the wrong motivator.

In Ezekiel, God describes these false shepherds: they didn`t bind up the wounded or care for the sheep. They steal the wool. They didn`t drive away the enemy, so they lost some sheep. They are cruel and abuse the sheep rather than care for them. Because of these types of leaders that covet and harm sheep to fill their covetousness. The sheep become a prey to the enemy because these false shepherds scatter sheep. It is a description of Israel under some bad kings. It is a description of some churches. God says He will fight against those false shepherds Himself. He will make them give account for the flock. They are held to stricter standards because of the leadership role.

In Ezekiel 34 God goes on talking about those false shepherds. He promises hope for the sheep. He says He will judge them, He says He will set up a righteous shepherd, someone with a heart of a shepherd like King David – like Jesus. There is a hope and promise for the Good shepherd who will bring blessings for the sheep, give them lush pastures and care for them, carrying the lambs. God promises a covenant of peace. He speaks blessings from the hand of a gentle, kind shepherd.

If you are in a congregation and the shepherd speaks and it doesn't speak to your spirit, you are not in the right church. I don't mean once or twice, I mean consistently. There is a local church where you fit. The church will fit like a glove fits your hand. The preaching will comfort, teach, inform and direct you. The worship will cause you to press into God. If this does not occur – you are not in the right church.

The shepherd speaks to his flock. They respond to his or her voice. I like to see it. God speaks through the shepherd to the people so they are nourished by the preaching or teaching the people are crying or excited or inspired to pray. It is something supernatural. It isn't just any preaching or teaching. It is God speaking through the voice of the shepherd to all the sheep at their particular level of need and giving them the best He has for them. There is a protection, a blessing, a feeding that is unique and God-ordained deep spiritual level.

Sheep know the shepherd's voice and O they respond to the shepherd's voice. He leads them by streams of water (Psalm 23). He gives them the nutrients that they need in a way that only God's anointed shepherd could give. The true shepherds of God won't be trying to take from the sheep. They will be trying to give something to the sheep. Jesus came to bring life and life more abundantly. King David as a shepherd fought against a lion and a bear to save his sheep. He has boldness and believes he can take on Goliath because of the LORD. He knows God can empower him to do whatever must be done. Jesus gave his life for us.

Knowing the seriousness of leadership and the influence a leader can have on his or her people should make us sober in our examination of our own hearts. We should be constantly examining our own hearts for motive. We should be praying that God would lead and direct us. Even if the Church votes or the board advises but there is a spiritual check in the leader's spirit – the leader should obey the LORD. There are so many ways to promote a seeker friendly, low threat gospel with watered down preaching as food for the sheep. These things are popular. There are companies that promote them and teach them promising more people will come- but what is the cost? Leaders should be led by the LORD, not by programs, or committees' recommendations.

God's Commands for Shepherds and Leaders

The churches usually met in people's homes, small groups – we would call them cell groups today. They met privately because they couldn't meet publicly. God gives specific direction to leaders and pastors. The shepherd always cares about getting the sheep to a pasture. The pastor should be praying about what to teach and preach knowing it is spiritually important for the congregation.

1 Peter 5: 1 I exhort the elders who are among you, as one who is also an elder and a witness of the sufferings of Christ as well as a partaker of the

glory that shall be revealed: 2 Shepherd the flock of God that is among you, take care of them, not by constraint, but willingly, not for dishonest gain, but eagerly. 3 Do not lord over those in your charge, but be examples to the flock.

God can give shepherds and pastors special words to bring to the people that will be life transforming. God can give a dream or a vision or an experience or a song. The pastor will know when he or she is being lead by the Spirit. Please notice the same warnings are repeatedly given throughout scripture. There is warning against covetousness or abuse. There is a command to feed and care for the sheep – for their spiritual growth and development.

In some churches, there are some shepherds who literally hold on to people and won't let them go elsewhere to be successful because the pastors know they have gifts and talents and don't want to lose them. They want to keep those sheep in their congregation. There are some who are jealous and fear losing that person or family so they don't promote them or send them out with prayer and a blessing. Their motives are selfish.

Once more a warning against covetousness – why? Because these people are entrusted with resources and finances. People trust them and give to them. That is why the shepherds must guard their hearts. God gives them the charisma and the wisdom to handle the resources and finances for the glory of God. They should not be covetous – money should not be their main motivator. God is their source of supply. If they view God as the source of supply, they will not be believing the congregation is there to pay them. A true pastor knows that God is the provider and will be lead by the spirit concerning decisions about the church. Humility is essential – to keep remembering that it is God is the One who called him or her and it is His anointing that empowers for service.

Character qualities are so important to God. Godly characters can't be purchased except with your life. You can not impart godly character. You can't earn it. You can only learn to obey God throughout experience with Him. As you press into Christ, you are transformed into His image and likeness. Only in a place of prayer and praise and worship and receiving the Word of God can you develop godly character.

The thing is you may not even recognize the development of the gift of leadership in yourself until after you have acted or spoken or done something. Then you will realize that God has most certainly transformed you. You know it is Him and nothing you could do on your own. The thing that is your part is to say yes to God repeatedly throughout your life for the rest of your life. That is what you promised when you were water baptized. Give yourself wholly to God that He might grow you in the fruit of the spirit.

Fruit of the Spirit in the Congregation

The Fruit of the Spirit should be evident in the leader`s life. The gifts of God given to a leader are for all of a life. God doesn't stop the gift. The fruit of the Spirit shows the type of tree you are. We can tell a tree by its fruit. We can determine the origin by seeing the fruit. You can see the type of shepherd the person is by the fruit of their life.

Fruit of the Shepherd is in the Sheep

If the shepherd is corrupt by any of the things I discussed in this chapter, that congregation will not have peace. The evidence of abuse is seen in the sheep. Sheep that are content and happy and peaceful are evidence of a good shepherd. You cannot fake fruit. You may pretend in front of people, but the Holy Spirit will reveal the truth. A good shepherd will have healthy sheep. The people will be cooperating together, joyful and involved in their church. If you are in leadership, ask God to inspire you to care for the sheep; pray for the sheep; minister by the leading of the Holy Spirit.

Galatians 5: 22 But the fruit of the Spirit is love, joy, peace, patience, gentleness, goodness, faith, 23 meekness, and self-control; against such there is no law. 24 Those who are Christ's have crucified the flesh with its passions and lusts. 25 If we live in the Spirit, let us also walk in the Spirit. 26 Let us not be conceited, provoking one another and envying one another.

9 MOTIVATION OF MERCY

The motivation of mercy is really the love of Christ. That is the best way to describe it. It is the love of Christ that so loves another person that you literally feel for that person as though it were yourself. Empathy is the closest word to describe it that I know of – that means to care so much that you literally feel it as though it were yourself. It is normal in families for there to be strong love bonds with deep caring.

Parents usually care for their children so much that they would sacrifice themselves for their children. That is the type of love that I am speaking of – a deep personal, intimate type of love – deeper than friendship love. The deepest caring, the caring, you cherish that person, you highly prize, value, care for that person. You care with the very essence of your life blood. It is as though you are connected. The motivation of mercy can experience that deep intimate caring for a total stranger. God will bring a person to you and you will care for and pray and give to that person.

An example could be that you are in standing in the church hallway and a pastor may come by and perhaps speak a word of scripture to encourage someone in mourning. Pastors are often motivated by mercy because that's what gives them the care for the sheep. Not only pastors have the gift or mercy. There are many Christians that have this gift.

In percentage to the other gifts, this gift is more common than others. An example of the ministry gifts towards a person who has lost a loved one would be: a prophet would give a word of hope to the person; a pastor would comfort and embrace; an evangelist might pray for healing or encourage the person to focus on Christ; a mercy would sense the hurt or the pain in the other person and in fact be attracted to that person because of it. The mercy will minister embraces, kind words, a listening ear and consolation. Any type of pain whether physical or relationship or any type of loss, the mercy will want to comfort that person. The mercy gravitates to them.

Mercy as Body Ministry

I would like to compare the ministry of those motivated by mercy like this; if you were using a hammer and banging nails and mistakenly hit your thumb or finger, immediately your own body would respond. You don't think about it; your first response is to examine the area with your other hand; usually, I suck that finger or thumb to try to relieve the pain. It's not terrible, but it is not ok. It is spontaneous, non-planned movements. All of your body reacts together to try to comfort that finger or thumb.

You will think of all the first aid that you know of – rinse the area, apply a cold ice pack or compress etc. all of your life would be focused on caring for that minor part of your body; why? The body seeks to protect itself. The body cares for all the parts of the body to be functioning to the fullest. What I'm talking about is that very thing; the mercy reacts in such a way to bring comfort and relief to the other parts of the Body of Christ.

The preservation of self is the main motivation of the human life: homeostasis. It is the life force within a person's essence that desire to live will do everything it can to make the body comfortable. So is the gift of mercy in the body of Christ – to bring all comfort to all the members of the Body of Christ. That is why there are so many of them in the Body of Christ because this gift is necessary – vital to the well-being of the church body. Part of the reason for this because Jesus said they would know us by our love for one another.

John 13: 34 "A new commandment I give to you, that you love one another, even as I have loved you, that you also love one another. 35 By this all men will know that you are My disciples, if you have love for one another."

At a Micro-Level

Let me re-examine that nick on the thumb or finger with the hammer at a micro-level or close up view. I talked about what a person would do to try to comfort that part of the body. At the blood level, the same thing is going on. If there is any bleeding, there are blood cells rushing to that area to set up a screen of coagulates to stop the bleeding. The body is at a deeper level trying to do something to preserve and protect at the cellular level. Skin cells start reproducing as soon as they can. There is comfort coming to the hand from within the hand itself – spontaneous response to preserve and protect and care for and stop the bleeding; after that immediate response – the body continues to repair itself with more tissues forming etc. It is really quite miraculous the way God made our bodies to heal and to preserve life.

What I am saying is literally within the Church there are people who act as they agents of healing. Some immediately respond to bring comfort and relief. Some bring hope. Some are encouragers; some are released later after the wound is not visible but continue to comfort and build up and strengthen the body so it can perform at an optimum level. The person motivated by mercy doesn't turn it off and on. It is a spiritual gift – the prompting is of the Holy Spirit. The person living in the spirit is led by the Spirit to use this gift.

Mercy is a Spiritual Gift

There is an error in teaching believing that those with the gift of mercy are operating in the soul or by his or her feelings. It is not an emotional gift; it involves the emotions. The mercy may actually cry with the one crying, but if that's all there is the person is in the realm of the soul and not in the spirit. The mercy will be prompted to listen, to pray, to speak words of comfort, to speak Scripture.

The mercy feels for the other person so strongly it is as if you are caring for your own self-preservation in care for the other person. No one can turn it on or turn it off by himself or herself. We can give ourselves to God and ask Him to use us but, the Holy Spirit is the director. The compassion of God motivates you to bring comfort to that person. It may include hugs, holding of the hand to comfort, kind words, serving the other person or giving in some tangible way. These are ways we comfort those who are in pain or in grief.

The words spoken by a Spirit filled mercy will be anointed by God to bring comfort. The scriptures spoken will be like a healing balm to the person. God's word will immediately go to the spirit part of that person bringing inner strength and healing. The mercy and compassion with the faith of God and the anointing of God impart comfort and healing. It is imparted. It is transferable: spirit to spirit. It may be hard to believe that it can be but it can be.

In Isaiah 40 God's word to a backslidden, sinful Israel is a word of comfort and forgiveness.

40 Comfort, O comfort, My people,
    says your God.

2 Speak kindly to Jerusalem,
   and cry to her
that her warfare has ended,
   that her iniquity has been pardoned,
that she has received of the hand of the Lord
   double for all her sins.

The best hope and comfort that can be given to a sinner is that Jesus paid the price for your sins. There is hope. God is reaching out to you. In Isaiah, the comfort is not only in the word be comforted but that God has forgiven you and will bless you. These are people who don't deserve any good thing from God, because they sinned, but God loves and cares and is in fact reaching towards them in love and mercy.

The word "comfort" itself coming from God brings comfort. Fear must be cast out so that love can bring the comfort to the person or people. Iniquity being cleansed is a comfort to the person or people also – at a deep spiritual level. This is a foreshadow to the Messiah Jesus who would come and cleanse them from all sins. This is spoken hundreds of years before the birth of Jesus.

Unconditional Love

I would compare this to perhaps a child who disobeys his or her parents; the child has misbehaved and has a bad attitude and is even disrespectful to the parent who is going to discipline his or her. This is a total situation of will against will. The parent chooses what is best for the child but the child is against the parent. It is as though in such a situation the parent says I forgive you. I want to comfort you. I am going to bless you twice as much as I was before. Only God can have that type of love. I know that parents love their children and that the love for a child is strong but only God can pour out such tremendous love that not only forgives but blesses and cares and even pays the penalty for the sin. That type of unconditional love is what overwhelms us. The mercy of God towards us wins our hearts.

The heart of God's love for us is that He keeps reaching out to us throughout our lives. He gives us opportunities to accept Him as Saviour and LORD. He keeps making ways, sending people, to try to teach us or lead us to Christ. He keeps trying to build bridges to us so we can accept Him. This is the mercy of Christ. As the coagulate chemicals rush to stop the bleeding finger or thumb within the hand, God is giving us opportunities to receive healing. The heart of the matter is He sees the root of the sin – it is not love. If we know the love of God towards us, we won't want to sin; we will want to rush towards God. We would know He has the best for us. He is not trying to stop us from enjoying life; He has a life beyond what we can imagine of joy, pleasure, fulfillment etc. God wants the best possible for us. God sees beyond the sin itself and sees the core need of our being to be filled with the love of God: His Holy Spirit filling us. He promises hope, not only restoration but a double blessing to let us know He wants to give us the best.

Ezekiel 18: 23 Do I have any pleasure in the death of the wicked, says the Lord God, but rather that he should turn from his ways and live?

God weeps at the sins of the people. His heart is passionate, loving towards every person on earth; those who accept Him as Saviour and LORD, and those who don`t. He loves the sinner as much as the saint. He shed His blood so that all people could be saved. God`s mercy is towards the wayward. If a Christian falls into sin, God does not stop caring. God`s heart is to reach out to those people to restore them. If someone falls into sin, we should do all we can to restore the person.

Restore Such a One

Galatians 6 Brothers, if a man is caught in any transgression, you who are spiritual should restore such a one in the spirit of meekness, watching yourselves, lest you also be tempted. 2 Bear one another's burdens, and so fulfill the law of Christ. 3 For if someone thinks himself to be something when he is nothing, he deceives himself. 4 But let each one examine his own work, and then he will have rejoicing in himself alone, and not in another. 5 For each one shall bear his own burden. 6 Let him who is taught in the word share all good things with him who teaches.

What About the Christian Who Sins?

We should realize the person`s sin is a symptom of a deeper issue – it is a spiritual issue. What is necessary is spiritual restoration. I`m not saying that there may not be consequences to someone`s sin, only that God is merciful. A teenage girl who commits sexual sin may be pregnant; a child could be her new responsibility. If someone breaks the law, that person may have to go to jail. There may be a consequence to the sin. That doesn`t mean that God stops caring for her or won`t care for them. A person who falls into sin must be restored. Leaders are held to a stricter standard. If someone in leadership sins, it is to be confessed in the congregation. It is part of the consequence. Please don't think that God doesn`t want to restore people who sin. Leaders who sin can be restored. Those people are often neglected or shunned. Often sheep scatter at such a thing. It causes some to doubt God or to make excuses for their own sins.

Restoration of a Leader

What is necessary is that someone spiritually mature come and speak hope, encouragement and restoration. There is a need for a figurative walking alongside the person as the person is restored. I mean a mature Christian or more than one should gravitate to the person and offer care. What is most often ignored is that the person who sinned has also caused a wound in himself or herself. You cannot sin and there not be a penalty. That is why we must be quick to repent. The person does not have to repent every day or beat himself or herself or anything like that. The true Charismatic church doesn't believe in suffering for our own sins; Jesus paid the price for all sin. Often these people are ignored after a sexual sin. What is most needed is that those who are spiritually mature, motivated by mercy but with wisdom, by the leading of the Holy Spirit, come alongside these leaders or people and restore them: invest time with them, invest spiritually in them, give them gradual responsibility until they are completely restored.

- This issue in itself could be the topic of a book.

God Cares

God knows our very being – He abhors the sin but loves the person. He understands what it is like to live on the earth because Jesus came and lived a Holy life on the earth. He was tempted but without sin.

Hebrews 4: 15 For we do not have a High Priest who cannot sympathize with our weaknesses, but One who was in every sense tempted like we are, yet without sin.

Spiritual Compassion

The compassion of Jesus moved him on the earth, He healed people. He fed people; He taught people; He raised the dead. The source of the miracles and healings was godly compassion for people. Notice that everywhere in the scripture where it speaks of compassion, it results in an action to relieve the situation.

Matthew 14: 14 Jesus went ashore and saw a great assembly. And He was moved with compassion toward them, and He healed their sick.

The Ultimate Mercy

The ultimate example of Jesus compassion led Him to die on the cross as He surrendered His human will the night before in the garden of Gethsemane. Even though he was human and didn't want to die, the only hope for mankind was if someone who was perfect, someone who was Holy, took our place and died for us. His compassion for us, made Him choose to suffer and die so that we could be restored to God, so that we could once more have peace with God and right relationship. It was our only hope.

Don't ever believe the lie that the compassion of the LORD is emotional. It involves emotions, because we are human – but the source is spiritual.

Compassion Moves a Mercy to Faith

Emotions don't heal anybody. I can cry for you and with you all day, but if I don't go beyond that, that is only human emotion. A true mercy motivated by the Holy Spirit may cry for you and embrace you but the Holy Spirit within him or her will compel him or her to apply healing through anointed scripture and words of wisdom or words of knowledge or prayer or some spiritual action. A true mercy operates in other gifts as required to bring the healing to that part of the body. Please know there are different levels of maturity. It is important that we are instructed about spiritual gifts so that we can learn. Submitting completely to the Holy Spirit, and learning from more mature Christians are also necessary ways we can learn to use our giftings with effectiveness.

Healing

The words of our mouth have to do with the person's healing. Part of the healing of people comes with anointed words. Most often it is scripture. Sometimes words of knowledge spoken can release healing in people also. The believers must use their authority to pray to bind up the broken hearted. I mean we believe it and pray it as though God were literally closing the wound as we speak. Faith in the words spoken is essential. Prayer is often the vehicle God uses – but prophetic words of encouragement are also effective. The important thing for the mercy is to obey the Holy Spirit. The Holy Spirit will quicken the words to us. Our faith is in Jesus – our trust is in Jesus. As we obey the Spirit, healing can be imparted.

Matthew 18:18 "Truly I say to you, whatever you bind on earth will be bound in heaven, and whatever you loose on earth will be loosed in heaven

.

Isaiah 61 is a Messianic prophecy that Jesus fulfilled. But Jesus has given us the authority and the responsibility to identify with these scriptures and live them.

61 The Spirit of the Lord God is upon me
  because the Lord has anointed me
  to preach good news to the poor;
He has sent me to heal the broken-hearted,
  to proclaim liberty to the captives,
  and the opening of the prison to those who are bound;
2 to proclaim the acceptable year of the Lord
  and the day of vengeance of our God;
  to comfort all who mourn,
3 to preserve those who mourn in Zion,
  to give to them beauty
  for ashes,
  the oil of joy
  for mourning,
  the garment of praise
  for the spirit of heaviness,
  that they might be called trees of righteousness,
  the planting of the Lord,
  that He might be glorified.

These words fulfilled by Jesus are the mission statement of Christians on earth. Jesus said as He was in the world so are we. (1 John 4: 17). We have the authority and the anointing to perform God's will. The same Holy Spirit that Jesus was anointed by resides in us. We should study the messianic scriptures not only as history of what Jesus fulfilled but for what we are to do on earth because we are the body of Christ. We should be identifying with Christ in ministry. We should do what Jesus did because we are followers of Jesus. He lives in us; He wants us to bring life and healing to other people.

A true mercy anointed by the Holy Spirit, will identify with Jesus in compassion and also in speaking words of faith and in actions that bring healing to people. He wants people to be healed and He is saying it can be imparted. If we are willing vessels, God will use us.

Identification with Jesus

Isaiah 61 gives us some objectives in ministry.

Vs 1 We should be communicators of the good news. We should not be declaring negative situations in the earth; we should be declaring good news of hope of being set free. The meek have hope. Jesus is their champion. There is someone who is on the side of the meek or the powerless: Jesus is the hope.

The words of our mouth can literally bring healing to the broken hearted. Just as a doctor might sow some stiches to help the healing of tissues, so can the anointed of the LORD speak words of faith that literally stich together those who are wounded. We can speak faith to them and bring hope to their lives. A person moved by compassion of the Holy Spirit can bring spiritual hope and life to people. What comes out of our mouth should be pure, should be holy. We should be given to speaking scripture – Oh yes, because the Word of God never returns void (Isaiah 55:11). We should be speaking the word of life into people's lives.

Our own words express kind thoughts and feelings, but God's Word has within it the power to bring itself to come to pass. God's Word spoken in faith can reproduce after its kind. It can cause a desert to blossom. The Word of the LORD is eternal and when spoken with a heart gushing with godly compassion and faith – it produces life. You literally say with the authority of Jesus Christ, " I bind that broken heart. I release healing and restoration and life." Literally you speak to the spirit of the person. If you do not stop it from being wounded – you will be pouring into a vessel that leaks. Whatever you do or say will never be enough. You must go to the root of it and speak healing.

Faith in the Word

Saying it alone without faith accomplishes nothing. If I say out loud "I am a fairy princess." It accomplishes nothing because I don't believe I am. The words have no power or authority. I know I am not. I am saying our words must align with faith in the word of God. God's Word is His will for us on the earth. God's Word has within itself the power to bring itself to come to pass. If you do not believe the person can receive a miracle– you can't impart. Go pray first – stir yourself up in the Holy Spirit and believe God can use you. God's Word isn't magic. God's word is eternal and living and when it is spoken with faith – it produces supernatural results. We must believe that the source is Jesus; He died on the cross to bring us salvation but also for our healing and for our peace and for our wholeness.

He Carried our Sorrows

Please know I have experienced the death of family members, dear cherished people. We can not let mourning dominate in our lives. We must stop the pain by binding up the broken hearted. If those loved ones are with the LORD, we should be rejoicing at their home going. We should be joyful for them. If you think of the loved one, thank God that you know he or she is in heaven,; Keep doing it; your thanksgiving to God will drive the sorrow out It doesn't mean we don't miss them. It doesn't mean we don't love them and wish we could be with them. Thank God for the good memories you do have of that person.

Thanksgiving and praise are keys to overcoming deep grief. Also, investing your life into others by serving or giving will help. It does mean that we commit it to the LORD. He carried our griefs and our sorrows – we don't have to give in to them. We should not be grieved as others are grieved.

What if we don't know those loved ones are with the LORD? Have the faith that your witness to that person mattered. Your sowing into that person's life made a difference. God is so merciful. Think of the mercy God has shown to you by bringing you to the saving knowledge of Christ. Trust that God's mercy was reaching out to that person until the last moment of his or her life.

By faith believe what Jesus has done for you. Believe Jesus is the healer. He is softening your heart for a person or people to pray for them. Jesus wants them whole and healed. If a person professes to be a healer – is none of the LORD's. Jesus is the Healer. That is our confidence.

The gifts of the Holy Spirit

Christians know that the gifts of the Spirit are in us but we realize these are gifts – not something we have earned. The Holy Spirit living within us activates the gifts and prompts us to use them. All the glory is to Jesus – all the supernatural healing, miracles, resurrection life – comes from the Holy Spirit. Christians know it is God and not ourselves who is the origin and who gets the glory. It's God who gave us the gifts, God who prompts us to use the gifts, and God who uses us as we minister the gifts. Christ in us the hope of glory. It is not of our own power – but by our obedience to the leading of the Hold Spirit.

Don't Stop with Feeling

The only part that could be from your soul is your initial connection with the grieving person or the person suffering loss. God will move us towards that person by attracting us to him or her. We may begin to weep – as we are feeling their pain. Please don't stop there. Nothing is accomplished if you stop there. What a mature mercy must do is pray. Cry out for God to help you to pray for that person. Expect that God will use you. We must speak words of life to end the pain. God will give us the words to speak and it will bring healing to that person. If you feel for people who are in mourning or grief or in pain, I mean you can literally feel it inside of you, it is not for no reason. You are a born again, spirit filled Christian so God wants to use you to speak healing into that person's life.

Righteous godly compassion, would compel us to press into God for a scripture or a word to pray for the person or people. Care to bring healing.

To Proclaim Liberty to the Captives

Good news for drug addicts or alcoholics is that they can be set free. Sexual addictions, pornography, any types of addictions – Jesus died to set these people free. There are people who cannot stop themselves; they can't help themselves – they are captives of their addictions. The good news for them is that they can be set free. Jesus Christ came to bring us life – and life more abundantly. His blood shed for us is stronger than any addiction.

Some addictions come off as soon as anointed words are spoken. I don't know why others linger in a person after he or she is saved. The solution is still the same. Jesus blood has set us free. We must preach and teach freedom from addictions. Some people only need to hear it once. Others may need a support group of Christians around them with prayer and love and constant truth of liberty in Christ being spoken to them and over them.

Deliverance to the Captives

The truth is Jesus Christ set you free. You accept Him as Saviour – receive Him also as LORD, knowing that the liberty from all addictions is for you also. Some may say it is for others nut not for me. That is a lie. You do not have to be addicted to anything. Start fixing yourself on Jesus. Start memorizing scripture. Start worshipping God more. Start praying more. How much do you want to be free from the addiction? That's how much you should press into Jesus. Gather with your local church. What are you prioritizing?

Most people who are addicted are feeding themselves all the wrong stuff. What are you listening to? Does it glorify God and bring peace and joy to your spirit? What are you watching? Does it encourage you to be more Christ like? Does it encourage you to want Jesus more? What types of magazines and papers are you reading or websites are you going to? Do they make you stronger spiritually? The truth is all these things can. If you go to the right places, you can be building yourself up and encouraging yourself and causing yourself to grow more like Christ.

Don't Feed on Garbage

You cannot tune into the negative news of the culture on an economic roller coaster, watch seductive sexual videos and pictures, listen to hatred and negative words, cursing and hearing blasphemy and feel peace. These things acceptable on most TV stations are totally unacceptable to your spirit. You were born from above once you were born again. Set your affections on things above (Col 3: 2). You can be set free but if you plug into all your old garbage sources of entertainment and recreation – you are like a pig who has been washed and cleansed and once released, goes back into his slop. The scripture says it is like a dog going back to lick up his vomit. The very thing that entangled you and ensnared you – you return to it. No. Don't live like that. You have been set free. Live like you are free.

It may mean new friendships. You may have to cut off all your old friends. If they are trying to get you to sin, you must cut them off. It very well might mean you must thrust yourself into Bible study and Christian life. Focus on Christ – get involved in your local church. Make some Christian friends. New life patterns will evolve and you will find yourself choosing right things instead of wrong things.

Some Mercies have Been There

Some mercies have testimonies of how the LORD has delivered them out of ungodly lifestyles or habits or addictions. I'm not against anybody reaching out in love to people with addictions. One less addicted person is always the best. I am saying you don't need to be content with a support group for drug addicts for the rest of your life. You should start identifying with Christ and seeing yourself as a new creation. You should start desiring things that encourage, things that edify, things that build up and encourage you. You should start wanting to serve Christ to share what God has done for you. You should stop wearing the label of drug addict or alcoholic and see yourself as a new creation in Christ – set free by Jesus to worship and praise and live free – because you've chosen Christ.

True love says you don't have to stay with that old label. Don't say about yourself "I'm addicted to…" Stop saying it. Start saying the Truth of God's Word. Jesus Christ has set me free. Who the Son sets free is free indeed. (John 8: 36). True love transforms you. No longer are you an addict. You are the free. You are the healed. You are a vessel God has placed His glory within.

To Proclaim the Acceptable Year of the LORD

You want some more good news to give somebody? Start preaching Now is the day of salvation or healing of deliverance of blessing of favour. You don't have to wait for it to manifest. Jesus paid the price over 2000 years ago by dying on the cross and being buried and rising from the dead victoriously. Today is the day to believe. You can not earn it. There is nothing you can do to make yourself more attractive to God. He already loved you with His life's blood while you were a sinner – long before you were ever born. He has proven His love by rising from the dead and saying that if you believe, you can be born again; you can be free; you can be victorious. New life is now. Don't go back – go forward.

The Lie that Sin is Best

I have spoken with some people who don't want to make the decision for Christ right now because they want to" live it up before they die and repent and accept Jesus at the end of their lives." They laugh "Ha ha". They actually believe the lie that sin is more pleasurable than living for God. It is a lie. You were not created for sin but to be filled with God's presence for God's glory.

They do not know the glory and the awesomeness of knowing Jesus. Loving Christ is the best possible thing for us. We were created to worship. We were created to live using our gifts and talents for God's glory. We were created to enjoy the pleasures of God. It is God's delight to give us the kingdom. In His presence is joy – beyond all earthly description or understanding. He wants to give us the best. The desires of our hearts can only be satisfied once we embrace Jesus Christ and the life He has for us. His idea of blessing us is so far beyond anything we could imagine on our own. His delight is in prospering us, causing us to bloom, causing us to grow and flourish.

If you hear someone who says foolish things such as I kind of like my life the way it is right now (drugs, alcohol, sin, breaking the law etc.) your heart should be torn and you should start crying out for God's mercy on that person's life. Pray for God to soften their hearts. Pray that God would give you words to speak. Pray God would target that person for the gospel that he or she would be saved.

God knows how to bless us beyond anything we can imagine on earth. You mate – your husband or wife cannot please you the way God can please you. There is no pleasure on earth that can compare to the glory of God in your life. In the depths of your spirit, you can accept what God has done for you. You can know pleasure and joy that goes beyond human comprehension. Jesus is the way, the truth and the life (John 14:6). Right now God is merciful towards you; won't you repent and give yourself to God? Without Him you can't be free.

The Oil of Joy

We can boldly proclaim to people whose lives are in shambles, wrecked by sin – you can be set free. You can have life. You can expect blessing and favour from God. How about Hosea's wife?

She sold herself into sin as a prostitute. She was abused and ravaged and left without one penny, naked and sold as a slave in the market. Hosea went to her and purchased her, clothed her and loved her and treated her kindly. He loved her as if she had never sinned. That's the type of love I am talking about here. I'm talking about supernatural love that comes from Jesus Christ – mercy that appoints beauty for ashes the oil of joy for mourning. Even if you yourself are to blame for your situation – His mercy is reaching towards you with forgiveness. Let the comfort of God's word speak to you. His love for you goes beyond anything you've done or could ever do.

Being thankful for the minor things and the large things, is essential to keep our hearts positive. Praising God throughout the day is a way to release the oil of joy in your life. We must know it for ourselves. We must teach it to those we minister to.

Beauty for Ashes

How can ashes be made beauty? New growth will come. Your life won't be the same. New joy will spring up with new opportunities and things so awesome you can't imagine. God doesn't just give you what you had; He gives you more than you can expect or even imagine. If it is a divorce or a relationship thing or the consequences of a sin or breaking the law – listen, the mercy of Christ is reaching out to you. It won't take once. It comes with constantly abiding with Jesus – getting to know Him more that you realize He loves you more than you ever could have known.

His presence fills you; His glory is in you and on you and God gives you opportunities to use your gifts and talents with others. You begin to see others receiving a blessing because God used it. You realize that God not only wants to bless you but He also wants to use you to be a blessing to others and to bring the good news of the gospel to others.

He loves you so completely; He loves you to wholeness – Oneness with Him. As you realize it is His love for you that is the core of His relationship with you, your spirit is quickened to new life. Jesus would never be satisfied with you almost healed. Jesus would never be satisfied with you mostly good. He would never be satisfied with you mostly restored. No. It wants to bless you with double compared to what you had. We must minister this truth to people. Don't let them believe the lie that they might have to live with anything less than total healing.

Isaiah 61: 7
Instead of your shame
   you shall have double honor,
and instead of humiliation
   they shall rejoice over their portion.
Therefore, in their land they shall possess a double portion;
   everlasting joy shall be theirs.

The Same Spirit

You may think to yourself, yes Jesus was the Messiah, He could do all those things. The same Spirit that raised Christ from the dead lives in you. The same anointing that was on Jesus can use you to minister life transforming love to people. Those of you moved by mercy, will immediately identify with this teaching. You will say "Oh it is me." If you start seeing people crying, it will move you to crying and wanting to comfort that person or persons. You will feel for that person. You say Yes

– that is me. The reason I'm writing this is not so that you'll know it is you, but so that you'll know the mercy is for a reason. It is to move you to faith. It is to move you to action to bring words of healing, words of hope, words of life to that person.

In prayer, I have felt it like an actual punch in my stomach where it hurts so much that I keep praying and praying for that person until it lifts. The feeling compels me to prayer. Sometimes it compels me to give, to take action etc. It is so essential that we obey the Holy Spirit. It is not for us to handle by ourselves. If we believe we can do anything to help the person without the Holy Spirit, it is a lie. If we believe we are the answer, we have nothing. We are obedient vessels. God can use us to show His divine love to people. We must not get caught up in the soul. The fleshly Christian cannot ministry pure mercy because he or she will get into pride, lust, boasting, any ungodly feeling.

Discerning of Spirits

I would give this word of caution in case you have any doubt about your relationship with the person who you are feeling the mercy for. You spend quite a bit of time with the person for a duration. Only God can determine this. It is not to be a crutch for the person but to be a support that encourages that person to heal and to grow. You may already be friends so it is easy. You may minister once to someone and never see the person again. If it is a new person, completely rely on the Holy Spirit to direct you in terms of what you should do. Do not be deceived into thinking you are the answer. You are being used by Christ to bring healing and wholeness. You may become close friends or not.

Stay out of the Flesh

Usually, it should not be with a person of the opposite sex – you must get someone to go with you if it is. It is best if men deal with men and women deal with women. Also Christian teams of two or more can minister together. The gift of mercy, because it is complete intimate love towards someone, can be misinterpreted by the person who is receiving. The person may think it is sexual or that he or she needs YOU. You must be mature and strong. You must be prayerful and pure in heart. Do not get over into the flesh. It is not you the person needs, but Christ.

Always pray for the person and ask God to lead you with direction. It could mean visitation and prayer and worship. The motivation I am talking about is spiritual. I am not talking about feeling sorry for someone. I am saying it should be clearly separate than your daily life – that doesn't mean you can't become friends. Let me give you an example of what I mean. The Pastor of the Church is the pastor but also has a wife or husband. It is completely inappropriate for the spouse to interrupt the pastor ministering to someone for some marital private matter and visa versa. The person you are ministering to must know that it is Jesus using you. Humility, meekness, pointing at Christ etc. are ways to make this known.

Assignments

I would liken these ministry opportunities as assignments. There are one meeting assignments. There are short assignments. There are long assignments. The longest one I've ever been on was 2 years. I could feel it like a punch in, my stomach. I would pray and pray and there would be a slight release. I did not stop praying until I saw manifested physical evidence of recovery. I can't say I don't still pray for those people because I do – but the heavy burden lifted once the person was healed. It involved so much intercession and separation in prayer and ministry.

The assignments usually involve listening, praying, caring, giving, praying, speaking the scripture etc. Your prayer for the person should be like an iceberg. You should do more unseen prayer and intercession for the person than what the person knows. It will keep you Christ focused and precise and keep you out of the soulish realm. Pray in tongues. Pray scriptures for that person. Pray alone. Submit prayer requests but mention no names.

Get all the prayer support you can. Just as you know you were assigned to pray for and minister mercy to someone, so will you know that you have been released. It will lift, as clouds are blown away leaving a clear sky, the same will occur. Pray until it lifts.

True spiritual mercy comes from the Spirit and it is ministered inspirit and its affects are spiritual and life transforming. God does comfort us and uses us to comfort others.

2 Corinthians 1: 3 Blessed be God, the Father of our Lord Jesus Christ, the Father of mercies, and the God of all comfort, 4 who comforts us in all our tribulation, that we may be able to comfort those who are in any trouble by the comfort with which we ourselves are comforted by God.

In the presence of the LORD no darkness can stay because the spirit is the leader of the soul. Only the Spirit can bind the soul. We can comfort them because God comforted us. There are ministers who have come from gangs and immoral, illegal positions. They were set free, they were delivered so they preach with conviction and authority knowing that if God could do it for them, He could do it for you. They have special mercy and compassion for people who are in the situations they were set free from.

Each thing we go through, including our assignments by the Holy Spirit can cause us to minister with more unction. The more we see the miracle working power of our God, the more we know He can do it again.

Romans 12: 6 We have diverse gifts according to the grace that is given to us: if prophecy, according to the proportion of faith;

Speaking by faith

If we are to speak by faith, what can occur? According to our proportion of faith – we can speak forth prophetically. It is not only for prophets alone but for those who have opportunity to minister. Speak from the faith of CHRIST who lives in you. Stir up yourself in the Holy Spirit until you can speak God's Word so that you know that you know that you know it is for now. You can speak life or death into people's lives. Are you moved with mercy? Don't speak death! Pray until you know you can face that person and proclaim God's word to that person. Don't nullify your gift by speaking what is – yes it is so horrible. What a tragedy. I hope you can get through – don't speak these words of unbelief or doubt or death into people.

Words of life

Speak words of life into people. Speak God's word with authority. The person most likely can't see it on his or her own. You be prayerful and speak the high way – the Word of God. It will cause that person to be strengthened inside. It will bring hope and healing. If you do not have a direct scripture – literally pray for a scripture. The least you can do – is speak "In the name of Jesus Christ, may hope come to you. Healing for your soul, your spirit your body...life to come...: speak some life into those people.

You have the choice to bring life to people. There must be faith activated there. You have got to pray so that the Holy Spirit will use you. Fasting and prayer could be necessary for both you and the person. Obey the leading of the Holy Spirit. Where do you measure your faith? Don't let it be in your own self or what you know. Let your faith be drawn from the life of the Holy Spirit who lives within you.

How big is your faith? Do you believe God is bigger than this situation for that person? If not, start praying in the Holy Spirit receiving from Him the faith that can raise the dead. If you know you are will someone in sorrow or mourning or is broken hearted, start praying in the Holy Spirit until the words or scriptures come to you. Start asking God for a word of wisdom or word of knowledge or a scripture. Speak life into the life of the other person. You can impart life. You can bind up broken hearted people. I am a living example of it. I know that I know that I know God can heal in such as way, it is as though it was only a distant shadow – with no pain.

If you do not have this type of faith to believe that God can do the impossible, start praying in the Holy Spirit. Start listening to teaching or preaching by strong faith preachers such as the Copelands, Joyce Meyer, Marilyn Hickey, Benny Hinn, Rod Parsley etc. Read books by Kenneth Hagin and T.L. Osborn, Smith Wigglesworth and the Hunters; It will inspire you to faith. Your faith level must rise if you are to help bring healing or deliverance to people. If you are not there, bring those people to someone who you know does believe in miracles.

The Good Samaritan

I believe I have emphasized that prayer is essential but I am saying that if the person literally is bleeding on the side of the road, we should do more. The good Samaritan is an example of this.
The Samaritan not only poured oil and wine into the person's wounds and wrapped them, he took that person to an Inn and paid so the person could stay there providing food and shelter for the person until the person was healed.

Luke 10: 33 But a Samaritan, as he journeyed, came where he was. And when he saw him, he had compassion on him, 34 and went to him and bound up his wounds, pouring in oil and wine. Then he set him on his own donkey and brought him to an inn, and took care of him. 35 The next day when he departed, he took out two denarii[c] and gave them to the innkeeper and said to him, 'Take care of him. I will repay you whatever else you spend when I return.'

Practical

He literally helped the person by doing practical stuff. We may need to get the person a place to stay, or help him or her to fill out papers or help with some practical thing. It is important that we obey this prompting as well. We need some church body ministry in some cases – practical food, clothing, a place to stay, etc. Some servants from the church could help. The pastor could offer encouragement. We are a body and not only one person should respond. We should care for the person as if for our own self.

Matthew 18: 18 "Truly I say to you, whatever you bind on earth will be bound in heaven, and whatever you loose on earth will be loosed in heaven.

We should take this scripture literally. Mercy is important. Indicators to know you have this gift is that you will literally feel what that person feels. You will gravitate to those people or that person. You'll care for them Some use this gift one on one- some open rehabilitation places for people who are coming out of prostitution or gangs. They help people overcome. Your feeling for them is only an indicator. It is not a solution. The solution can only be found through prayer asking God what is the solution. If you don't have a scripture start praying what I can do to help this person?

What we focus on is what we treasure. Start praying for that person and God will start showing you ways to minister to that person, giving you scriptures. Don't stop until you know there has been healing. You must build up your own spirit so you can minister to people. True ministry brings immediate comfort by hugs and prayer but also healing and deliverance.

CONCLUSION

Words of Encouragement for You

In this study of the motivational gifts of the Holy Spirit, we have discussed scriptural examples of the gifts, the cautions and the tips for success. It is my prayer that you will have learned about your spiritual gifts and been inspired to care to develop your gifts by pressing into God and asking Him to use you to serve within the Body of Christ.

May God use you to build up and strengthen and encourage parts of the Body of Christ around you in your local church. May God use you to connect with other Christians beyond your local church to glorify Christ in your city and province or state and country,

May God link you to mature people who have similar giftings who can help you to grow and mentor you in the faith. May God use you to mentor others.

May God grow you in the fruit of the Spirit. May God use you in the gifts of the Spirit.

May you give your life as a living sacrifice unto God (Romans 12: 1-2) so He can use you.

Let the awesomeness of Christ's love compel you to prayer and action.

Let the Word of God be a priority in your life.

May God cause you to know you were created for a purpose larger than you can possibly know. May God use you as a clean vessel set apart for God's glory.

May God grow you in prayer so that you may recognize the promptings of the Holy Spirit and obey. May God develop in you the manifestational gifts of the Spirit. I pray it for you. You also pray it for yourself. God, I stir these gifts:

Gift of Faith, gift of working of miracles, gifts of healing

Gift of prophecy, gift of tongues, gift or interpretation of tongues

Gift of word of wisdom, gift of word of knowledge, discerning of
 spirits

Should God call you in a ministry gift as Apostle, Prophet, Evangelist,
Pastor or Teacher, May God give the education and training both academic
and spiritual so that you will be effective in ministry.

May God use you to win people to Christ, to heal to deliver to bring
hope and life to people.

Give God the glory; keep your heart pure so that God may use you
throughout your life.

ABOUT THE AUTHOR

Chris Legebow is a Christian Professor of English and Communications. She has taught at the elementary, high school and College and University levels. She has ministered in her local churches in intercessory prayer, teaching Sunday school and other Christian Doctrine classes to children and youths. She has preached to congregations and given her testimony. Although she was not raised in a Christian home, she came to know Jesus Christ as her Saviour and LORD while she was studying in University. This radically transformed her life in terms of priorities and commitment.

She has a strong passion for the great commission – that Jesus Christ would be preached throughout all the earth believing that it a major sign of the LORD's return. She has been a part of several different types of full gospel charismatic churches but has also gained much of her insight and enlightenment from Christian Media and broadcasting. She hopes to continue ministering, serving, interceding and giving and teaching until the LORD returns.

www.ingramcontent.com/pod-product-compliance
Lightning Source LLC
Chambersburg PA
CBHW020039040426
42331CB00030B/66